POSITIVE CARERS

The Rights and Responsibilities of HIV-Positive Health Care Workers

Paul Mayho

CASSELL

Cassell
Wellington House
125 Strand
London WC2R 0BB

127 West 24th Street
New York
NY 10011

First published 1996

British Library Cataloguing-in-Publication Data
A catalogue record for this book is available from the British Library

ISBN 0–304–33275–5 (hardback)
0–304–33277–1 (paperback)
Typeset by Keystroke, Jacaranda Lodge, Wolverhampton
Printed and bound in Great Britain

POSITIVE CARERS

Also available from Cassell:

R. Bor and I. Scher *Introducing Systematic Therapy*
M. Jacobs (ed.) *The Care Guide*
H.-J. Schulze and W. Wirth (eds)
Who Cares? Social Service Organizations and their Users

Contents

For Tony Machin

Foreword

HIV infection is an emotive subject even without the unnecessary scaremongering of the tabloid press. Place the subject of HIV infection within the context of health care provision and the issues are not merely emotive but of real human concern for those working within the profession and members of the public who want to be able to trust that the Health Service consistently provides the highest standards of care and safety.

This book discusses the rights and responsibilities of HIV-positive health care workers. It looks at the issues an infected worker may face and takes into account the existing guidance on the management of such workers. Written in the light of current transmission risk data, the book sets out to demonstrate that many opinions are based on misinformation and prejudice and that the rights of infected health care workers are sometimes compromised because of this prejudice. It also examines the portrayal of HIV-infected health care workers in the British press and how this has affected the predicament of the HIV-infected health care worker. The book includes quotes and comments from a variety of sources which reflect the broad range of attitudes towards HIV-infected health care professionals and suggests possible strategies to promote awareness and tolerance.

A variety of readers will find this book useful. For students it provides an informative basis for project and/or degree work. It can be used by occupational health departments as an aid to the better understanding of the predicament of HIV-infected health care workers; in fact everyone in the health care profession will find this book interesting and relevant. The book is also a useful and accessible reference source for journalists.

The Department of Health has asked me to make it clear that the complete text of its guidelines on the management of HIV-infected health care workers is not included in the book, though it is quoted from at length. It can be obtained by writing to:

BAPS
Health Publications Unit
DSS Distribution Centre
Heywood Stores
Manchester Road
Heywood
Lancashire OL10 2P2

Positive Carers is divided into two parts. The first details the facts relevant to HIV-infected health care workers, looks at the rights and responsibilities of HIV-infected health care workers and offers a solution to challenge current thinking. The second part is more general and explores the myths, attitudes and public comments about HIV-infected health care workers. The appendices contain excerpts from official documents from the Department of Health and the UKCC.

Preface

The stresses and strains for anyone who discovers that they are HIV-positive are many. But for the health care worker the ramifications of a sero-positive HIV diagnosis are unique and are an added strain to the usual ones a newly diagnosed person may face. I am a former HIV-infected health care worker. I found the strain on my career, the prejudice I faced and the misunderstanding of my disease too much to deal with all at once. By the time I resigned, six months after diagnosis I felt ready to die then and there; indeed I felt dead already.

After about two years in a complete wilderness, and feeling rejected by my own caring profession, I decided to use my personal experience to try to change the attitudes HIV-infected health care workers face. I had noticed in the newspapers that the dilemma of HIV-infected health care workers who continued to practise in the knowledge of their status was being widely debated. The tabloid press reported stories of AIDS time bombs roaming the nation's hospitals, a potential lethal menace to patients.

I contacted a professional magazine, the *Nursing Times*, and I met their special correspondent, Daloni Carlisle, who wrote two features on my story. These features resulted in my attending the Royal College of Nursing Congress in Harrogate in 1993 and a consequent media flurry around the subject of HIV-infected health care workers. At the same time the news of a nurse who was charged with murdering several of her patients with insulin broke in the press. The nursing profession was shaken by the Beverly Allit case. It could not have happened at a better time for the tabloid press, who took the opportunity to twist the knife a little more using HIV-infected health care workers to further damage the trust the British public have in the National Health Service and its workers.

It seemed that I was the first HIV-infected health care worker to speak openly to the press. This was an experience. I clearly remember journalists virtually salivating at the chance to talk to me and I experienced at first hand how newspapers sometimes misquote people and even how they could fabricate stories or, at the very least, heavily embellish them. Deterred and disillusioned by the behaviour of the press, I began to feel like giving up again.

That was until one day a letter was forwarded to me by the *Nursing Times* (one of the publications that didn't make anything up) from Sue Morris who had seen some of the articles. I agreed to meet Sue and we hit it off immediately. A few months later Sue and I set up Give Way, an organization to act as a listening ear to HIV-infected health care workers. We were turned away by every funding body we approached, but we decided that this was too important to abandon and we set it up with our own money. We ran the help line from Sue's front room.

In the first few months our suspicions were confirmed; the calls were coming in thick and fast. The creation of Give Way triggered more interest and I started to speak publicly on the conference circuit all over the country about the dilemma of HIV-infected health care workers, mainly speaking about my personal experience of discrimination in the workplace.

During this time I also began to study the rights and responsibilities of HIV-infected health care workers. It had become a personal crusade and I felt sure that if I worked hard enough something good might come out of the rubble of my own life and in some small way this dreadful experience might have been worth it. In June 1994 I began work on this book and it was accepted for publication by Cassell. I spent the next year-and-a-half researching and writing the book. I found that although there was information on the subject, most of it was scattered and difficult to locate. There was nothing in one handy volume. I have incorporated much of my findings here in an attempt to remedy this.

Whilst writing this book my HIV status became an AIDS diagnosis when I had a bout of PCP in August 1994. I discovered a whole new aspect to my disease, having trudged along for a few years being relatively asymptomatic with HIV. My AIDS diagnosis did come as a shock and the feelings I went through were similar to those when I received that initial HIV diagnosis. I was surprised because I thought I had already worked through the personal issues around the illness in those two years I spent in the wilderness. A paradox of my AIDS diagnosis was the motivation it gave me. I pursued my studies with renewed vigour.

So that is basically how I came to write this book. Researching it has also helped me to create a philosophy on HIV and AIDS, which I would like to share with you to illustrate my politics on the subject.

As a gay man living with AIDS I have become more concerned about the actions and motives of a few individuals and HIV organizations. When I hear phrases such as the 'AIDS industry' and the 'HIV mafia' I wonder what I am part of as a person living with AIDS.

It upsets me to think that although there are many in the 'HIV industry' whose motives are honourable, their hard work and dedication is marred by those who appear to be using the tragedy as a trendy launch pad for their own personal and political agendas. In my observations of the HIV industry I have found a varying response. It ranges from those who would agree with the above statement on motives to those who agree and don't want to be quoted, to those who staunchly deny there is any agenda other than HIV prevention.

Before I go any further I would like to make a distinction between HIV prevention and AIDS prevention. As there is no known cure for HIV or AIDS at present our primary defence must be to stem the transmission of the virus. HIV-prevention programmes in this context are a good thing. AIDS, a potential stage of HIV disease, is not as well programmed or funded as HIV prevention. In effect, you can expect far less from organizations if you are already infected. I can quote the Gay Men Fighting AIDS minutes of June 1994 as an example which clearly states that the second aim of GMFA, 'To minimise the harmful consequences of infection with HIV for gay men', is not being addressed due to reasons of 'time and energy', 'funding being HIV prevention led', and the issue of the aim being 'forgotten'. However, since then GMFA have designed a strategy to minimize the harmful consequences of HIV.

Any mention of HIV and AIDS as an industry raises, for me, an uncomfortable feeling that I am merely a commodity, a small piece of something much larger. If this is so, having shares in the industry, so to speak, should entitle me to something, even if it is just to be listened to. But it seems that there are many uninfected shareholders who hold the balance of power. My voice is a silent murmur in the hubbub of a gigantic machine. Daring to challenge these uninfected shareholders only brings calls of 'heresy'.

Organizations or individuals that call for individual empowerment should realize that we the 'commodity' have the right to scrutinize their actions and agendas. I interviewed Ceri Hutton, Chair of the UK Forum on HIV and Human Rights and asked if she believed that HIV was being used by some merely as a platform for personal gain. She said, 'Yes, people can have personal agendas which coincide with professional agendas, which is not necessarily wrong as it motivates people. The danger is that personal agendas can run away, ceasing to be open to scrutiny and challenge.' She went on to tell me that she didn't think that the voices of people living with HIV and AIDS were being listened to enough.

In an industry where money is being used primarily for HIV prevention rather than AIDS prevention, people like me are left feeling like a lost cause. Instability amongst the ranks of the uninfected shareholders, driven by personal agendas and the desire to make a name for themselves out of the rubble of other people's lives, could destroy any further chances of funding and influence the choices of those in power.

I believe that it is vital that HIV-infected people are heard in order to stop any such disaster and to help those who slip through the HIV-prevention net and become fully fledged HIV-infected shareholders. After all, it is those who are infected who give the industry its reason to exist.

So why is it that the HIV industry seems to listen so little to its infected shareholders? Is this because the industry is in trouble? I think not, for the self-appointed directors of HIV plc would never have been so stupid as to build their careers in a company that was about to go bust.

Whilst doing my research I came across an article titled 'Why John is angry'. It was about three men all called John who had founded an organization called the UK Coalition of People Living with HIV and AIDS, an organization of, by and for people infected with the virus. I felt for the first time that I had found an organization I could work with. I had worked independently for two years, because the other HIV and AIDS organizations I had approached did not want to know. I had found the HIV sector uninterested and unhelpful.

I feel very angry about the fact that most of these organizations were set up by people who were infected themselves, and having fought and won many battles, have died away and have been replaced with what can only be described as AIDS careerists, non-infected HIV people who have used the HIV agenda to further the causes of gay politics.

Although at present HIV mainly affects gay men, we know that it also affects many other groups such as intravenous drug users. I believe that HIV has been affecting people since the mid 1970s. Those affected were mainly IV drug users and at the time the illness was termed 'junkie flu'. We didn't know about HIV at that time. When gay men started to die and the first organizations were set up in the early 1980s, the people behind it were white, wealthy, middle-class, educated gay men. The HIV sector hasn't changed much since, except for the fact that the early pioneers have almost all died and have been replaced by the great uninfected. People like myself who are already infected do not seem to have a place in the HIV-prevention world of the AIDS industry in Britain at this time.

The 1994 Paris Declaration signed by 42 heads of state clearly advocates the need to involve people who are infected with the virus. Most HIV organizations said that the declaration wasn't worth the paper it was written on. However, the UK Coalition of People Living with HIV and AIDS felt differently about the Paris Declaration. The members believed that the infected have a key role to play and for this reason I felt I could work with them.

The UK Coalition of People Living with HIV and AIDS has provided me with the resources to pursue my work and for that I am grateful. At the time of writing we are implementing a nationwide project to dismantle regional differences in the standards of care for people with HIV and AIDS and to challenge the attitudes of health care workers towards those with the virus. The project uses a peer advocacy model devised by Sarah Grice. (It is presented in Chapter five.) I am most impressed by the model, which takes an old idea and gives it a fresh approach, using HIV-infected health care workers to educate their peers. Such a project has ramifications for the caring profession and, if proven to work, it could be taken into many other areas of disease. Such a move is in keeping with the Paris Declaration and I believe it is a wonderful way of using a resource that is so far under-used and often completely wasted.

I have found myself in a strange situation in terms of my work. On the one hand there is the medical fraternity, and on the other there are the AIDS activists. Both have different philosophies. Whilst the health care fraternity is more pragmatic about HIV, I have found some activists have a romantic view. I cite as an example an ACT UP America member at a human rights convention who approached me after a remark I made to a speaker who was a little confused about the risks of an HIV-infected health care worker continuing to practise. It is very difficult to mention the dilemma of the HIV-infected health care worker without mentioning the case of the Florida dentist who is said to have infected five of his patients. (It is discussed in some detail in Chapter 3.) The activist was incensed that I had mentioned it at all saying that it was merely a propaganda weapon produced by the Center for Disease Control (CDC) in Atlanta. I realize that the Florida case is a very emotional one for many activists, but the fact remains that it seems likely that the dentist infected five of his patients. DNA strand testing would suggest this was the case, although the actual mode of transmission is unknown. As long as AIDS careerists and activists use the HIV epidemic as a platform for their own political agendas the voice of those infected will be lost and, along with the media, will only serve to cause further confusion about the transmission routes of HIV. We must not let this happen.

Thankyou to the friends and colleagues who helped, particularly Carol Pellowe of Thames Valley University.

Paul Mayho
June 1996

Part One:

Rights and Responsibilities

Introduction:
HIV in the health care setting

Sue Morris, SRN Dip N

Throughout history humanity has struggled against plague and pestilence, its successes and defeats shaping the socio-economic structure of civilizations today (Open University 1986). However, as people strive to develop cures and to conquer disease, it is unlikely that they will ever succeed in eradicating all harmful organisms from the environment. Indeed, just as mankind was getting used to the idea of effective control over bacterial infection through the miracle of antibiotics, there is growing evidence of more virulent strains of bacteria which have genetically acquired resistance to multiple drugs. For example, in the US a strain of tuberculosis has been observed which is resistant to virtually all the available antibiotics. A relationship based on an inter-dependency between humans and micro-organisms exists, with one achieving dominance over the other for varying periods throughout history.

In the absence of cures, we have sought to alleviate the symptoms of disease and to provide care and attention to those afflicted. It has been as a direct result of this management of care that improvements in prognosis have been made, and realistic understanding of the course of a disease has been achieved.

The general public, in their fear of contracting HIV, have been quick to react negatively to the inability of science to 'tame' the virus. Certain groups directly affected by HIV have rightly advocated on behalf of the infected, showing the inadequacies of care and the mismanagement of related illnesses. Government funding policies have been criticized and horror stories of 'AIDS victims' have reminded us all that there is no room for complacency in the world we share with HIV.

Nevertheless, we must not lose sight of the tremendous steps forward we have made because of HIV, and there have been many. It seems unsavoury to applaud ourselves on our achievements when so many continue to die, but there have been spin-offs concerning care and treatments that have benefited the population as a whole. Some examples are the revision of infection control policies; the recognition of nurses' roles as health educators (patients need to be openly and adequately informed of their medical diagnosis and its implications); and the acceptance of the voluntary sector's expertise working alongside statutory organizations. HIV has played a major role in these innovations to the benefit of all areas of health care, and has successfully promoted the benefits of a multi-disciplinary team philosophy.

The nursing profession has been criticized for being slow to develop care for people with HIV-related illnesses. However, in all fairness, HIV has provided nurses with challenges quite beyond the usual format of illness and disease.

Issues related to advocacy, confidentiality, the use of unlicensed therapies for symptom control and, above all, nurse–client relationships have succeeded in radically changing the concept of nursing for many within the profession. It has also served to highlight nurses' attitudes towards patients, particularly those who belong to groups primarily affected by HIV, namely homosexual and bisexual men and intravenous drug users both male and female.

The transmission routes favoured by HIV illuminates social behaviour previously identified as 'deviant' by society. For some nurses this endorses their own prejudices, encouraging discrimination against individuals based on their membership in that group (Niven 1992). So those who are HIV-positive often feel isolated from society and from the care givers to whom they turn for support. Awareness of personal attitudes and prejudices is therefore an important consideration for nurses.

An HIV-positive health care worker experiences this same sense of isolation, for discriminatory attitudes often prevent open disclosure of their status. Consequently, possible support from colleagues and the profession is not forthcoming. Problems surrounding supporting colleagues are not confined to HIV. Health care workers have often viewed the acceptance of support as a weakness, upon which they will be judged. This is because as individuals within a patriarchal and authoritarian health system, health care workers, and nurses in particular, are looked on with reverence by the public. Bond (1988) tells us that 'A nurse is often expected to be the solid idealized parent figure, the rock upon which those around her can base their stability'. An HIV-positive nurse may be identified as a weak link in the chain, through which increased supervision and even accusation may enter the profession.

It is important not to confuse discrimination with valid concerns for the health and safety of both the patient and the individual member of staff. In order to ensure that nurses' concerns are motivated by the latter they must scrutinize their own attitudes towards those primarily affected by HIV. Our paths through life are influenced by a diversity of personal experiences and, for some, the pain and difficulty of changes in attitude impedes success. Yet, the process of recognition that derogatory attitudes do exist deserves to be acknowledged.

HIV is here for the foreseeable future and as the number of those infected increases, so too will the number of HIV-infected nurses. Individual nurses have a responsibility to themselves and to their colleagues to maintain the integrity of the profession, and in so doing, to eradicate outdated attitudes that directly conflict with respecting an HIV-positive person, whether nurse or patient.

References

Bond, M. (1988) *Stress and Self Awareness: A Guide for Nurses*. London: Heinemann Nursing.

Niven, N. (1992) *Health Psychology*. London: Churchill Livingstone.

Open University (1986) Chapter 4: Infectious disease and human history. In *Medical Knowledge: Doubt and Uncertainty*. Milton Keynes: Open University Press.

Scott, C. (1994) *Care and Treatment of People with HIV Disease and AIDS: A Nursing Perspective*. London: RCN.

CHAPTER I

Issues and ethical implications

Rules are meaningless if people's attitude towards someone with HIV is not a very positive one.

The Economic and Social Impact of AIDS in Europe.

There are responsibilities that are relevant to all health care workers irrespective of HIV status. We are all duty bound to obey strict ethical and legal codes, because of the responsibility we have to patients to ensure their safety at all times. This chapter will examine the main issues and ethical implications, with reference to the guidelines written on the subject of HIV-infected health care workers. The guidelines are presented in more detail in the Appendix.

The primacy of the interests and safety of patients is the integral thread of the UKCC (United Kingdom Central Council) and Department of Health guidelines on the management of HIV-infected health care workers. Both sets of guidelines refer us back to the Code of Professional Conduct and remind us of our obligations and responsibility to the patient to 'act always in such a manner as to promote and safeguard the interests and well being of patients and clients' (UKCC, 1991). Effective care can only be provided if patients feel safe and trust those caring for them.

The risk of transmission of HIV from workers to patients is, in reality, much lower than the risk of transmission from infected patients to staff. However, a scan through the stories in the British press in recent years reveals an almost hysterical preoccupation with HIV-positive health care workers. Tabloids and broadsheets have questioned the risk to patients when HIV-infected health care workers continue to practise in full knowledge of their status. They have not reported the facts surrounding the risks or otherwise of being cared for by an infected health care worker. They have instead undermined the trust in health care workers and have therefore damaged the environment of trust that is required for effective care.

Bearing in mind the obligations and personal responsibility we as health care workers have to safeguard the interests of individual patients, how does a practising health care worker infected with the HIV virus risk the safety of individual patients?

The UKCC guidance states: 'Provided general infection control measures are followed scrupulously the circumstances in which HIV could be transmitted from a health care worker to a patient are restricted to exposure prone procedures' (UKCC, 1994). Even in the event of an HIV-infected health care worker carrying out exposure-prone procedures, with the implementation of universal precautions the risk is considered so small as to be only hypothetical. Stopping known HIV-infected health care workers from carrying out exposure-prone procedures is possibly an overreaction, as there must be health care workers who are carrying out exposure-prone procedures who are HIV-positive but unaware of their status. The fear of the potential risk of HIV transmission from a health care worker to a patient does not really justify targeting only known HIV-infected practitioners, as the guidance tells us that all practitioners pose a potential infection risk. The risk of transmission is so neglible that no one is known to have been infected by a health care worker in this way. The UKCC's guidance concerning HIV-infected health care workers states:

The occupational risk of HIV transmission from a practitioner to a patient is very remote in any event, but negligible if appropriate practice methods and strategies are diligently followed. Such precautions amount to no more than the good clinical practice which all practitioners have a responsibility to maintain in all situations, irrespective of their serological status and knowledge they have of their patients. All blood and body fluids pose a potential infection risk and appropriate precautions must be taken. (UKCC, 1994)

The guidance goes on to say that 'safety comes through recognizing that all practitioners, like all patients, pose a potential infection risk'. There is no such thing as a suspected HIV-positive patient if they have not been tested. It jeopardizes the safety of both the patient and the worker to think otherwise. To assume that a patient is infected because of their sexuality is in the first instance dangerous and in the second discriminatory. The guidance tells us that all patients pose a potential infection risk, and the same is said of practitioners. Therefore all practitioners should maintain high standards of clinical practice and diligently follow universal precautions in caring for all patients. It might be said that being prejudiced against certain social groups could seriously damage your health. In a report funded by the Department of Health on nursing and AIDS, two-thirds of nurses interviewed said that their colleagues were not adopting recommended infection control procedures for all patients (National Federation for Education Research, 1993). The report also indicated that many took precautions only for patients known or suspected of being HIV-positive.

Safety must be ensured by all health care workers, not just for the safety of the patient but for themselves also. It is therefore every health care worker's duty to realize that safety depends on their own actions and not necessarily those of the patients. Safety comes from a degree of control over the working environment, an environment where universal precautions are diligently observed by all. It is every health care worker's duty to ensure that safety. If the Department of Health and UKCC guidance policies are a knee-jerk reaction to HIV-infected health care workers it is only in the interests of safety.

RESPONSIBILITY OF THE HEALTH CARE WORKER

This section explores the moral and ethical responsibilities of HIV-positive nurses in relation to their patients, their colleagues, their employers and themselves. Through this process it may be possible to identify areas which need addressing when initiating policies which govern HIV-positive health care workers, in order to ensure that the health and safety of the participants in care are observed and protected at all times.

Tschudin (1986) stated that the moral duty of nurses is concerned with the recognition of a 'threat' which needs to be prevented, whereas the ethical duty of nurses concerns the ideals that need to be pursued. The ideal might therefore be interpreted as ensuring patients' safety whilst being cared for by an HIV-positive nurse, but in order to achieve this the moral code of the individual is at the centre of conduct. The two are inextricably linked.

The ideal would require that all nurses uphold truth and retain their integrity, even if such action resulted in evidence, detrimental to the individual, being brought against them. However, nurses are only human and are subject to the same emotional and financial constraints as the general public; they can easily fall victim to self-protecting, personal motivation.

The underlying reason for concealing the truth is usually fear. Fear of one's actions or incompetence being discovered, fear of publicity, fear of punishment, fear of future implications. In the case of HIV, a positive nurse is placed in the unenviable position of being infected with a virus which is both socially discriminated against and has implications for her or his clinical practice. Fear plays a major role in decisions following diagnosis.

Fear of being discriminated against is certainly a component in the decision-making of nurses. The health care setting is not exempt from prejudice and it can occur on a ward as surely as it can occur in any other social environment. Niven (1989) describes prejudice as an attitude towards someone in a social group which leads to a 'negative evaluation' of that person, simply because they belong to that group. This is often displayed in a subtle manner which is hard to confront, and leads to stresses reflecting suspicion and distrust on both sides. An HIV-positive nurse is likely to be identified as a member of a group 'at risk' from HIV, which society has already labeled deviant. They are seen to have obviously participated in activity which has led to their infection. This colours the attitudes of their colleagues, and affects the way they are treated after disclosure. In order to address this situation the term 'innocent victims' of HIV has crept into nursing vocabulary, separating those who have been infected by needle-stick injuries, occupational exposure or transmission through use of blood products from those who contracted the virus sexually or from IV drug usage.

Whilst some AIDS activists and trainers advocate that HIV does not differentiate and that all members of society are at risk from infection, the fact remains that there are three definite modes of transmission. However, human curiosity being what it is, speculation will continue about other possibilities. Various surveys have indicated that nurses are still ignorant of the facts surrounding HIV, and that in the absence of knowledge, fear generates an atmosphere of prejudice and discrimination. In order to encourage disclosure of an HIV status the social climate should ideally be sympathetic to such diagnosis. If it fails to be receptive, concealment of status could be seen as a favourable alternative by HIV-positive nurses.

Whilst information provides nurses with the knowledge they need to plan strategies in care it is not merely facts and figures that dictate what that quality should be. HIV is a disease affecting society's moral concept and nurses need to explore their own attitudes and beliefs in order to gain insight into what is meant by quality care for people living with HIV. This two-pronged strategy in HIV education needs to be addressed by nursing educationalists if positive nurses are to openly reveal themselves to colleagues and employers.

With Department of Health approval of general nurses and nursing students continuing in clinical practice with a well monitored HIV status, the burden of public disclosure has fallen on those who have undertaken exposure-prone procedures. Despite the assurance of the Department of Health that such exercises are undertaken only in circumstances warranting extreme caution, the media publicity that has followed disclosure has destroyed any sense of trust that the Department of Health's guidance had previously generated. It is therefore an area in need of much consideration concerning policies governing HIV-positive health care workers.

The concept of 'look-back' exercises is based on ensuring that patients have not been inadvertently placed at risk by infected health care workers during exposure-prone procedures. The ideal is that at all times, regardless of status, a nurse ensures that there is no mutual transference of blood between carer and patient. However, accidents do happen, and although policies governing universal precautions and accident procedures are set up to protect both parties, situations occur whereby nurses fail to notify the proper authorities. Lack of time, concern or awareness of the possible dangers and the fear of repercussions can all motivate a nurse to conceal accidents.

The UKCC *Code of Professional Conduct* (Appendix C) is quite clear that nurses should not purposefully conceal anything that might be detrimental to their patients (UKCC 1991). However, nurses are also governed by law: a nurse who acts in this way can be charged with negligence.

> Negligence is the omission to do something which a reasonable man, guided upon these considerations which ordinarily regulate the conduct of human affairs, would do, or to do something which a prudent and reasonable man would not do. (Blyth v. Birmingham Water Works, 1891)

A nurse must therefore accept that she is legally as well as professionally bound to disclose both accidents during exposure-prone procedures and her HIV diagnosis to the appropriate agencies (specified in the Department of Health Guidance). Ignorance of the law does not exclude her from responsibility. Indeed any physical or psychological damage caused to an individual by her omission may result in financial awards to that person. This has major implications for employers and has been responsible for many of the calls for mandatory HIV testing of nurses in the United States.

The decision to inform a patient that they are currently or in the past have been cared for by an HIV-positive nurse, needs to be carefully considered. At the present time it is undertaken by consultation with the AIDS Advisory Board of the Department of Health, and only in situations where exposure-prone procedures have been involved.

Public disclosure of an HIV status is not seen to be a requirement of nurses, indicating the likelihood that the general public are currently being cared for in a professional manner by many HIV-positive health care workers without any problems.

However, disclosure of a nurse's HIV status to colleagues has to be seen as a personal choice based on the circumstances at hand, otherwise breaches of confidentiality and intrusion of privacy could well be cited by nurses, against colleagues. Ideally the nurse should be supported by the Occupational Health Department or the Director of Public Health, and advised on this sensitive issue; and it is vital that these agencies are fully equipped to advise in a competent yet sympathetic manner. It is for this reason that trusts and hospitals have an obligation to their work-force to explore the issues related to HIV-infected health care workers, gaining expert advice where necessary in order that they can formulate a workable policy based on the Department of Health's Guidance within the health care setting.

It is vital that 'One must not mistake the enemy by fighting against the infected person instead of the virus' (Khailat, 1993), or that scaremongering practices of the media do not influence the judgement and skills of health care professionals. It is obvious that at the end of the day the responsibility for safe practice is down to the individual nurse.

Nurses must be absolutely clear that their motivations are within the boundaries of their Professional Code of Practice and the law. When in doubt they must obtain advice from statutory bodies in order to safeguard their own and their patients' position within the health care setting. Whilst the path might not always appear to be fair, the nurse's duty is quite clear and there is little room for deviation. It is also the duty of all nurses to ensure that they play their part in raising awareness of HIV and developing strategies to support and care for those affected, in order to 'normalize' the infection rather than uphold it as a stigma in society.

HEALTH OF THE WORKER

The Department of Health's Guidance on the management of the HIV-infected health care workers states that, 'For the benefit of their own health all infected health care workers should receive regular care from a physician experienced in HIV' (Department of Health 1994).

Naturally the good health of the HIV-infected health care worker is very important and a necessary requirement to continue working. The physical health of all of us determines to a degree the things we can and cannot do. As the HIV virus progresses, the health care worker may become more susceptible to infection. Hospitals being the places that they are, are essentially bug traps! Wards full of people with a myriad of complaints and diseases sometimes line badly ventilated rooms all breathing the same air along with the health care workers and other staff and visitors.

Professor Robert Pratt, author of *AIDS: A Strategy for Nursing Care*, tells us that

Workers with impaired immune systems resulting from HIV infection or other causes are at increased risk of acquiring or experiencing serious complications of infectious disease. Of particular concern is the risk of severe infection following exposure to other persons with infectious diseases that are easily transmitted if appropriate precautions are not taken (e.g., measles, varicella). (1994)

A prime example of this, and a frightening development in the world today, is the emergence of multi-drug resistant tuberculosis (Pratt, 1994), which is transmitted in the same way as drug-susceptible tuberculosis, i.e., water droplets manufactured by coughing. Multi-drug resistant tuberculosis and HIV together are associated with a high mortality rate. You are more likely to contract multi-drug resistant tuberculosis if you are immuno-compromised. HIV-infected individuals should not be exposed to this, particularly the multi-drug resistant form (Pratt, 1994). Therefore, being aware of one's HIV status could be an advantageous safety factor in protecting one's health. Health care workers who are unaware they are positive might find themselves in situations or working in environments that are unsuitable for them. The Occupational Health Service should be able to provide the HIV-infected health care worker with information about the risks that they may face, though they can only do this if they are aware of the health care worker's status in the first place.

'Any worker with an impaired immune system should be counseled about the risk associated with providing health care to persons with any transmissible infection' (Department of Health, 1994). In the case of a health care worker on a contagious diseases unit, redeployment would most certainly be necessary. But what of the unsuspecting health care worker who is unaware of their status?

The personal health of the health care worker is as important as the overriding ethical duty to the care of patients. The UKCC guidance states that 'A nurse, midwife or health visitor who believes that he or she may have been exposed to infection with HIV, in whatever circumstances, should seek specialist medical advice and diagnostic testing' (UKCC, 1994). It is all very well asking health care workers to have an HIV test if one suspects being exposed to the virus, but for this to be effective one must feel safe enough to have a test in the first place. Stories of health care workers going to the occupational health department like lemmings and being 'medically retired' when they are fit or being fired or forced to resign do not encourage health care workers to come forward.

It is little wonder that health care workers might think twice before telling their employer. As well as our overriding ethical duty to patients to have a test if we believe we may be HIV-positive (Department of Health, 1994), we face the same consequences as the general public when having or thinking of having a test. The Terrence Higgins Trust *HIV/AIDS Handbook* states that 'Sometimes the idea of taking the test is served up to us in media coverage of HIV issues as a socially responsible move' (Tavanyar, 1992). However, the effects of a positive result dramatically change one's life and most of us spend much time thinking about how we might deal with a positive result before taking the test. Is this a luxury afforded to health care workers?

When weighing up the pros and cons of having an HIV test, the treatment of HIV-infected health care workers in the past and past breaches of confidentiality can be black marks on the negative side of one's ledger. For those living in hospital accommodation the loss of a job may also result in the loss of a home. And for students suffering financial hardship, the loss of income, together with the loss of both career and home may have tragic consequences. The *News of the World* reported a story about two HIV-infected male nurses who made a suicide pact after contracting HIV in July 1993.

However, despite the hardship and discrimination one may face being HIV-positive, because of the nature of the virus and the deteriorating effect it has on one's immune system, it is sensible for health care workers to be aware of their HIV status in relation to the working environment. Many HIV-infected health care workers will eventually suffer deteriorating health and will have to be medically retired at some point. It is often pointed out that HIV can lead to neuro-psychiatric disorders and this might be good reason not to allow HIV-infected health care workers to continue working. The World Health Organization has come to the following conclusion:

> Governments, employers and the public can be assured that based on the weight of available scientific evidence, otherwise healthy HIV-infected individuals are no more likely to be functionally impaired than uninfected persons. Thus HIV screening would not be a useful strategy to identify functional impairment in otherwise healthy persons. Furthermore, there is no evidence that HIV screening of healthy persons would be useful in predicting the onset of functional impairment in persons who remain otherwise healthy. (Sieghart, 1989)

The question is, at what point should an HIV-positive health care worker be medically retired and who should make that decision?

THE ROLE OF THE OCCUPATIONAL HEALTH SERVICE

The occupational health department is responsible for ensuring that workers are fit to work. Ultimately any decision on the future employment of the HIV-infected health care worker would be taken here. Nine paragraphs of the Department of Health Guidance on the management of HIV-infected health care workers are devoted to the role and responsibilities of the occupational health service. The first paragraph states in part that 'All matters arising from and relating to the employment of HIV-infected health care workers should be coordinated through a specialist occupational health physician.' (Department of Health, 1994).

In assessing whether the HIV-infected health care worker can safely continue with work, the competency of the worker, area of practice (e.g. are exposure-prone procedures involved?) and health of the worker will be considered.

The Department of Health guidelines state that they 'apply to all health care workers and students in training, whether in the public or private sector'. As a qualified health care worker, one is expected to be competent in terms of clinical practice. But it cannot be said that student health care workers are fully competent to work as qualified members of staff. For example, a ward would not be staffed entirely by students; there would be at least one fully qualified member of staff to intervene where it was not safe for the student to do so on their own. The nature of, for example, a midwife's training requires the student to become competent in many areas of that specialty. To become competent enough to qualify, the midwifery student will have to learn how to perform what may be termed 'exposure-prone procedures'. These should not be carried out by HIV-infected health care workers (Department of Health 1994).

For some students an HIV diagnosis may spell the end of their career. This does not encourage a student health care worker to come forward in the light of an HIV diagnosis or even to be tested in the first place, as is expected by the guidance. On the duties and obligations of HIV-infected health care workers the Department of Health guidance states that 'students accepted for training should be apprised of such guidance, which applies to them during training, and will ultimately have implications for their future career.'

The type of practice that the positive health care worker might be expected to undertake and whether that practice involved exposure-prone procedures should be looked at on an individual basis by a specialist occupational health physician. Modification of practice or even removal from an area of practice may be required.

As stated earlier, many HIV-infected health care workers will eventually suffer deteriorating health. The decision as to when a health care worker is not fit to work should be taken by an occupational health physician. How might a specialist occupational health physician assess the health of a worker in relation to HIV? HIV attacks specific cells in the body. In particular it is attracted to the lymphocytes of the immune system, i.e. the T4 cells. By counting the circulating T4 cells in the blood a clinician can ascertain approximately how long a person has been infected and the viral stage of the infection. The average T4 count is between 500 and 1200, although 500 is a low average. When the T4 count drops just below 500, opportunistic infections may start appearing, such as oral candida or folliculitis. These are often the first indications for those who have never been tested that there might be something wrong with the immune system. As the viral load grows so the T4 count decreases and the type of infection may become more serious and even life-threatening. The health care worker may also become more susceptible to infections other than opportunistic ones. By American standards when the T4 count drops below 200 it is classified as an AIDS diagnosis. It would be sensible to say that when an infected health care worker reached a point where the T4 count was lower than 200, the worker should no longer work in the ward environment because of the risk of infection from patients. It is quite possible of course that the worker may decide on a medical retirement before this point because of fatigue and other symptoms of HIV disease. Many are quite symptomatic even though their T4 count is above 200. On the other hand there are those with no T4 cells at all who talk about leading fulfilling lives.

Another cause for concern is that of AIDS dementia. This course of the illness affects the minority rather than the majority. We know for sure that HIV is attracted to certain cells in the brain. Some newspapers have capitalized on this fact and suggested that demented nurses might be roaming our hospitals. This is incorrect: all demented health care workers get promoted to senior management when their dementia is recognized. Actually that is not true at all, but I couldn't resist it. I make light of it because it is one of the greatest fears of those who are positive, including myself. HIV can affect the brain at any phase in the progression of HIV. Anyone who shows signs of mental deterioration should be stopped from working immediately.

Occupational health departments need to be very clear about what is required of them by the Department of Health guidelines and should be aware of the course of HIV illness. They should be able to draw a realistic line as to when a health care worker becomes unfit to work. An unrealistic response to the HIV-infected health care worker and misunderstanding of the course of the disease could result in an inappropriate decision being made about the health care worker's suitability to work.

CONFIDENTIALITY

The concept of confidentiality is not restricted to the physician's office or to a managed carer organization, but extends to the workplace. Who has the right to private information and for what purpose? The issue of confidentiality has raised eyebrows among ethicists and medical providers for years. Medical information is confidential information. By definition, confidentiality means private, secret (Sacks, 1994). I believe that a confidential environment is a vital component to the Department of Health's and UKCC's guidelines on the subject of the HIV-infected health care worker. Both of them stress the importance of confidentiality. Confidentiality could be described as anonymity and, like the subject of responsibility, it has moral, ethical and professional connotations.

Nearly every hospital would say that they practised strenuous methods to ensure the confidentiality of all their patients. Indeed, the Government's Patient's Charter stresses this very fact. Privacy is a human right and is recognized under international law. The problem occurs in the case of the HIV-infected health care worker when people deem that confidentiality should be broken in the interests of public safety. It is easy to see how many people's own fears and misconceptions about HIV along with an inadequate knowledge of transmission routes could lead someone to break another's confidentiality, often, in all honesty, from good motives rather than bad ones. However, there are those who are so prejudiced that their motives are unquestionably bad. The tabloid press have time and time again released details of health care workers' names and addresses when reporting about them. Any such action from a health care worker acting on patient information would not be tolerated. However, the tabloid press hide behind the respectable screen of justifying their actions in the public interest.

If a breach of confidentiality could save another from being infected with HIV then I would say that the question of professional confidentiality would have to be examined. Yet the risk of HIV transmission from a health care worker is so small it is negligible and does not justify this course of action. So what is the problem?

The problem is that misunderstanding of the transmission routes and infectivity of HIV has distorted people's assessment of risk. Based on inaccurate information and fearful for themselves and others, they believe they are committing what essentially is a good deed by breaking another's confidentiality in the interests of others. As I have said earlier effective care can only be based on trust and such breaches of confidentiality can only serve to erode this trust, particularly the trust of health care workers themselves who fully know from experience that patient confidentiality is often an ideal that fails, and patients know this. A 1994 survey published by *Behavioral Health Management* stated that approximately 25 per cent of all Americans believed that their medical information had been improperly discussed during medical claims and transactions, and nearly 65 per cent were concerned that their medical information was being seen by organizations other than those providing health care. Sixty-five per cent also thought that computers were implicated in the unauthorized release of their medical records.

The examination of practices with regard to confidentiality should take place on an ongoing basis. As technology advances, particularly in relation to the handling of information, health care professionals need to stay abreast of developments. One of the problems is that although health care workers have a concept of medical confidentiality, those handling the information may not share that concept. The health information and personal details relating to HIV-infected health care workers for the moment should simply be kept under lock and key and separate from other medical information. Such a display of commitment to confidentiality can only strengthen the government policy on HIV-infected health care workers. Rigorous maintenance of confidentiality is critical to the success of the public health efforts aimed at preventing the transmission and spread of the HIV virus. If confidentiality is proven to be effective in protecting the identities of those infected, including health care workers, it can only be a good thing and help in the fight against HIV.

In common law, confidentiality is a moral obligation without legal enforcement. Of course the protocol for patients' records is widely known. The Patient's Charter states, on the subject of medical records, that 'Every citizen has the following established National Health Service right . . . to know that those working for the NHS are under a legal duty to keep their contents confidential'. Members of the medical profession are required by law to observe confidentiality. This goes beyond common law and in this context is legally enforceable. We can call this 'medical confidentiality'.

Reams have been written about 'confidentiality' and all of us, whether health care worker or not, have some concept of it. To understand it in the context of health care and the guidelines, we should first look at what medical confidentiality means to the medical profession. The Hippocratic Oath states, 'All that may come to my knowledge in the exercise of my profession or outside my profession or in daily commerce with men, which ought not be spread abroad'. The Hippocratic Oath is not taken by nurses, although they are expected to 'Hold in confidence all matters coming to his/her knowledge, in the practice of his/her profession, and in no way violate this confidence'.

In the context of being 'personally accountable', can disclosure of an HIV-infected health care worker's status be justified 'in the wider public interest'? In respect of other health care professionals known or believed to be HIV-positive the UKCC stated in their 1993 guidance that

> Nurses, midwives or health visitors who know or believe a fellow practitioner, whether within their own profession or not, to be infected with HIV but refusing to comply with professional practice should consider the council's expectations of them set out in the Code of Professional Conduct which apply at all times and in all circumstances. In taking any consequent action they would be fulfilling not only their duty to patients but also to their colleagues. (1993)

A registered nurse, midwife or health visitor is personally accountable and must 'Ensure that no action or omission' on their part or within one's sphere of responsibility 'is detrimental to the interests, condition or safety of patients and clients' (UKCC, 1991).

The UKCC statement was widely condemned by many for its use of the words 'know' and 'believe'. Some feared that the use of these words might cause a witch-hunt. In March 1994 the UKCC published its new guidelines and dropped the paragraph completely. The UKCC stated in a letter attached to the revised position that, 'In view of a number of developments since that date, the document has again been reviewed. The further revised edition replaces Registrars Letter 12/1993 which should now be destroyed'. (1994).

The Department of Health's guidance (1994) states that,

> In balancing duty to the patient and the wider duty to the public, complex ethical issues arise. As in other areas of medical practice, health care workers may be required to justify their decisions. The need for disclosure must be carefully weighed and where

there is any doubt the health care worker may wish to seek advice from his or her professional body.

Personal accountability and the need for disclosure must be carefully weighed.

As a registered nurse, midwife or health visitor . . . and in the exercise of professional accountability, [one must,] acknowledge any limitations in your knowledge and competence and decline any duties or responsibilities unless able to perform them in a safe and skilled manner. (UKCC, 1991)

Referring back to the original question of justifying disclosure in the wider interests of the patient and the general public, several things need to be taken into account. They are:

1. The statistical risks of transmission of HIV from an infected health care worker to a patient. (There is not one recorded case in Britain at the time of publication.)
2. The duty to ensure the safety of the patient at all times.
3. The compliance of *all* health care workers to practise good infection control measures at all times.
4. The required abstention by HIV-infected health care workers from carrying out what are deemed as 'exposure-prone procedures'.
5. Is the practitioner 'known' or only 'suspected' of being HIV-positive?

The Department of Health guidance (1994) states clearly with regard to exposure-prone procedures that 'Such procedures must not be performed by an HIV-Infected health care worker'. The guidance goes on to state that:

A nurse, midwife or health visitor who believes that she or he may have been exposed to infection with HIV, in whatever circumstances, should seek specialist medical advice and diagnostic testing, if applicable. She or he must then adhere to the specialist medical advice received. Each practitioner must consider very carefully their personal accountability as defined in the Councils Code of Professional Conduct and remember that she or he has an overriding ethical duty of care to patients.

In effect the responsibility is a personal one. It is up to the individual practitioner to disclose their HIV status or to seek diagnostic testing if appropriate. Disclosure of another health care worker's suspected status is not a justifiable disclosure. However, a registered nurse, midwife or health visitor must 'acknowledge limitations' of knowledge and 'decline any duties or responsibilities unless able to perform them' (UKCC 1991). If one is aware of a known HIV-infected health care worker carrying out exposure-prone procedures one must bear in mind the Code of Professional Conduct which states that a registered nurse, midwife or health visitor must 'Report to an appropriate person or authority any circumstances in which safe and appropriate care for patients cannot be provided' (UKCC 1991). This is a justifiable disclosure and is within the remit of one's personal responsibility.

The subtle differences depend upon one's own perception of people with HIV and possible prejudices that may go with it. All nurses in the exercise of professional accountability should 'maintain and improve their professional knowledge and competence' (UKCC, 1991). The practitioner should be aware of what comes within the context of their professional responsibility rather than what is brought on by their own personal prejudices.

Another possible breach of confidentiality occurs in the situation of a 'look-back exercise'. This is when patients are notified that they may have been exposed to a risk of transmission of the HIV virus during an exposure-prone procedure by an HIV-infected health care worker. The decision to carry out a look-back exercise is taken by the local director of public health and the UK Advisory Panel on AIDS. The Department of Health guidance (1994) states: 'The circumstances in which such a look back exercise should take place will vary with each individual case, depending on the specific working practices, skill and state of health of the worker concerned'.

Of course this is a rare event; it causes much distress to the public and is only ever put into action if deemed necessary. Naturally the media always take an interest in such exercises and have in the past ferreted about, often successfully, for the HIV-infected health care worker's identity. With regard to confidentiality at the level of the media, the Department of Health state in their Practical Guidance on Notifying Patients, 'Where a worker waives his or her right to confidentiality, authorities should take great care to prevent further information about his or her whereabouts being made generally known' (Department of Health, 1993).

If a health care worker has reason to believe they are positive they should seek HIV diagnostic testing and inform the occupational health department of the result. If an infected health care worker is not involved in exposure-prone procedures and they are healthy there is no reason for them to discontinue practising. If an infected health care worker is involved in exposure-prone procedures they should cease practising immediately and follow the advice given to them by their occupational health department.

It is every health care worker's responsibility to be fully aware of their obligations and responsibilities as defined in the UKCC's *Code of Professional Conduct* and to adhere to them. Failure to be aware of the Code is a beach of the Code's requirements.

MANDATORY HIV TESTS FOR MEDICAL STAFF

The prejudice of many is not based on risk factors or statistical evidence; it is based on fear born from ignorance. Research has been conducted by Access Opinions Ltd. (AOL) among the political opinion panel of 100 MPs, representative of the overall composition of the House of Commons in terms of party, region, marginality of seat, length of service and age. Although MPs are elected representatives, I do not believe that they reflect public opinion. I expect the public would be far more severe. A poll carried out in the United States indicated that 90 per cent of people would not make use of the services of a known HIV-infected health care worker (USA National Commission on AIDS, 1992). The AOL survey was carried out between 19 March and 13 April 1993; it was included in a presentation to the Terrence Higgins Trust and is unpublished. It was designed to gauge the gut reactions of MPs to simple questions on the issue of HIV-infected health care workers, which shows only a slim majority were in favour of mandatory testing. The following question was posed:

Q. There have been a number of cases recently of medical staff who have been infected with the HIV virus. In the light of these cases would you support mandatory HIV tests for medical staff?:

	Lib Dems %	Con %	Lab %
Yes	57	62	48
No	41	37	50
Don't know	2	1	2

Base: All MPs plus division by party.

The mandatory testing of health care workers is unethical and unworkable. A negative result equates the absence of antibodies to the virus being found in the blood sample at the time of testing. This does not rule out the fact that the health care worker may be in the 'window period' stage of infection and may develop antibodies a week later. Only a positive result can guarantee a person's HIV status. Standard pre-test counselling ensures a test candidate is aware of the fact that the antibodies are usually produced between three to six months post-infection (in very rare cases it may take a year or more) (Tavanyar, 1992).

There are many ethical implications of mandatory testing. In the first instance the decision to have the test should be one of choice rather than enforced. The Department of Health guidance on the management of HIV-infected health care workers supports the view that health care workers have a responsibility to both themselves and their patients to ascertain their own status in relation to personal behaviour risks, as previously noted. However, it is not unknown for occupational health departments to persuade health care workers to have the test based on their sexuality, which reflects a stereotypical view of who is at risk from HIV, and who is not. It must be accepted that HIV does not differentiate between gender, age, or creed.

It is probably the cost of mandatory testing that has acted as a deterrent rather than the ethical problems involved in enforcing it. It is estimated that one-time testing of all health care workers in the United States could cost as much as $250 million and as much as $1.5 billion for testing all patients (USA National Commission on AIDS, 1992). However, it is almost certain that if moves were made in Britain to employ mandatory testing of health care workers for HIV the Royal College of Nursing and members of the nursing profession would publicly denounce the motion and fight it.

MANDATORY DISMISSAL

One of the other questions posed in the AOL survey concerned the mandatory dismissal of HIV-infected health care workers. Once again I am uncomfortable with the assumption that MPs reflect 'public opinion'. Based on the reaction of the British press and the American poll revealing that 90 per cent of people wouldn't want to be treated by an HIV-infected health care worker it is safe to suggest that the public would support the mandatory dismissal of those found to be infected.

Q. There have been a number of cases recently of medical staff who have been infected with the HIV virus who continue to stay in their posts after discovering that they have contracted the virus. In the light of these cases would you support the mandatory dismissal of medical staff found to have the HIV virus?:

	Lib Dems %	Con %	Lab %
Yes	22	35	2
No	71	62	88
Don't know	7	3	10

Base: All MPs plus division by party.

The result of this question would appear to endorse support of HIV-positive health care workers, dispelling the profession's own fears that such practitioners would reduce the public's faith. (It is with thanks to AOL that these extracts from their survey are reproduced.)

The United Kingdom Declaration on the Rights of People with HIV and AIDS states that 'No person should be barred from employment or dismissed from employment purely on the grounds of their having HIV.' However, it should be pointed out that this Declaration is not an official document. The Terrence Higgins Trust and Royal College of Nursing are amongst the signatories, but it is not recognized by the British government. Workers' rights, however, are a crucial issue and require greater protection. A nurse who has been found to be jeopardizing patient safety through neglect obviously should be disciplined. However, if they have followed the guidelines as set out by the Department of Health and the UKCC there is no need for them to be disciplined on the basis of their status alone. If a medical examination has shown the nurse to be unfit for work then a second opinion should be sought, as the clinical expertise of one doctor may be compromised by lack of specialist knowledge. Expert advice must be stressed as part of the management of HIV-infected health care workers.

References

Department of Health (1993) *AIDS/HIV-Infected Health Care Workers: Practical Guidance on Notifying Patients – Recommendations of the Expert Advisory Group on AIDS*. London: DoH.

Department of Health (1994) *AIDS/HIV-Infected Health Care Workers: Guidance on the Management of Infected Health Care Workers*. London: DoH.

Goss, D. and Adam-Smith, D. (1995) Preconditions for policy development: workplace attitudes towards HIV/AIDS. In *The Economic and Social Impact of AIDS in Europe*. London: Cassell.

Khailat, L. (1993) Law and AIDS: issues and objectives. *Medicine and Law*, **12**, 3–10.

National Federation for Education Research (1993) *Nursing and AIDS: Material Matters*. Slough: NFER.

News of the World (1994) Nurses in AIDS Death Pact. 31 July.

Niven, N. (1989) *Health Psychology*. London: Churchill Livingstone.

Patient's Charter (1992) London: Department of Health.

Pratt, R.J. (1994) *AIDS: A Strategy for Nursing Care*, 4th edn. London: Edward Arnold.

Sieghart, P. (1989) *AIDS and Human Rights: A UK Perspective*. London: British Medical Association.

Tavanyar, J. (1992) *The Terrence Higgins Trust HIV/AIDS Book*. London: HarperCollins.

Tschudin, V. (1986) *Ethics in Nursing*. London: Heinemann Nursing.

UKCC (1991) *Code of Professional Conduct*. (2nd edn) London: UK Central Council for Nursing and Midwifery.

UKCC (1993) Registrars letter 12/1993. Annex 1 (AIDS & HIV Infection).

UKCC (1994) Registrars letter 4/1994. Annex 1 (AIDS & HIV Infection).

USA National Commission on AIDS (1992) *Preventing HIV Transmission in Health Care Settings*. Washington: The Commission.

CHAPTER 2

Fundamentals

No other disease has caused such emotional, prejudicial and often hysterical reaction as AIDS.

Susan Hart

SETTING THE SCENE

The public concern about HIV and AIDS has altered over the past decade. The earlier media coverage concentrated on HIV infection contracted by gay penetrative sex, intravenous drug use, haemophiliacs infected by the blood plasma product, Factor 8 and contaminated blood transfusions. Now media sensationalism has moved away from these subjects, perhaps because blood is screened for the virus and safer-sex campaigns initiated by the gay community have altered the course of HIV transmission. Or perhaps they are no longer newsworthy topics. However, HIV-positive health care workers are increasingly being portrayed by the media as a 'high risk' and a danger to the public. Media attention has switched to this new group, while maintaining its original sensationalism and inciting the same fears.

In the early days, the fear of contracting HIV from a contaminated blood transfusion was justified. Potentially, any one of us may find ourselves in the situation of requiring a blood transfusion as the result of an accident. We may not even be conscious when the procedure takes place and we know that people in the past have been infected this way. However, today all blood in Britain is screened for the HIV antibody and potential donors are questioned concerning 'risk activities', thus reducing the risk of transmission. A comparison can be made with health care workers. Society has a greater chance of coming into contact with a health care worker than having a blood transfusion. Therefore, just as donors have a responsibility to the public to ensure they honestly respond to the questions posed by transfusion centres, health care workers in the absence of mandatory HIV testing must also be honest.

It is important to emphasize, in the light of publicity concerning HIV-infected health care workers, that whilst large numbers of people can cite unscreened blood products as the transmission route for their HIV infection, *not one case of a health care worker transmitting the virus to a patient has been recorded in Britain.*

The welfare of patients is paramount and as health care workers we are required to maintain standards of professionalism and safety. These standards are set by the Department of Health and the United Kingdom Central Council (UKCC) for nursing and midwifery. The UKCC is an amalgamation of nine different nursing, midwifery and health visiting bodies which were dissolved as the Central Council and the National Boards assumed their full functions under the Nurses, Midwives and Health Visitors Act 1979 (UKCC Annual Report, 1984). The UKCC has four main functions:

1. To establish and improve standards of training and professional conduct for nurses, midwives and health visitors.
2. To determine rules for registration and maintain the single professional register.
3. To provide guidance for the profession on standards of professional conduct.
4. To act through the appropriate committees to protect the public from unsafe members of the profession. (UKCC Annual Report, 1984)

The Department of Health and UKCC are united in their policies on the management of HIV-infected health care workers. The contents of both the UKCC and the Department of Health guidelines are compatible and indeed the UKCC position statement refers in detail to the Department of Health document. (The UKCC statement is reproduced in Appendix B.)

The Department of Health Guidance on the Management of HIV-Infected Health Care Workers 1994 was written with consultation and includes statements from the General Medical Council, General Dental Council and the UKCC. The guidance, which contains the recommendations of the Expert Advisory Group on AIDS to the Department, applies to all health care workers and students in training whether in the public or private sector.

The Expert Advisory Group on AIDS was set up in 1991. They are also known as the 'panel' and are referred to as such throughout this book. In 1993 its remit was extended to consider health care workers infected with all blood-borne viruses. The tasks of the 'panel' are:

1. To establish and update as necessary criteria on which local advice on modifying working practices can be based.
2. To provide supplementary specialist occupational advice to physicians of health care workers infected with blood-borne viruses, occupational physicians and professional bodies.
3. To advise individual health care workers or their advocates how to obtain guidance on working practices.
4. To advise Directors of Public Health on look-back exercises in respect of patients treated by HIV-infected health care workers and also to advise on look-back exercises in respect of patients treated by Hepatitis B e antigen-positive health care workers.
5. To keep under review the literature on occupational transmission of blood-borne viruses and revise guidelines as necessary. (Department of Health 1994)

The panel is available to be consulted when the general guidelines in the Department of Health document *AIDS/HIV-Infected Health Care Workers: Guidance on the Management of*

Infected Health Care Workers, cannot be applied to individual cases or when health care workers or their professional advocates dispute local advice or where special circumstances exist (Department of Health 1994).

The UKCC position statement draws attention to the 'Code of Professional Conduct for the Nurse, Midwife and Health Visitor' which is a statement to the profession of the primacy of the interest of patients and clients. The Code emphasizes the ethical imperative faced by each individual nurse to serve the interests of the patients and clients through all their decisions and actions.

In summary, the Department of Health guidelines are the recommendations of the Expert Advisory Group on AIDS which apply to all health care workers and the UKCC position statement is based on the Department of Health recommendations but deals specifically with professional nursing issues.

ACCOUNTABILITY AND RESPONSIBILITY

The UKCC states in its Code of Professional Conduct (Appendix B), 'As a registered nurse, midwife or health visitor, you are personally accountable for your practice' (1991). 'Accountability' is generally said to mean that one is liable to be called on to give an account of responsibility. The definition of responsibility is generally thought to mean that one is morally accountable for one's actions, is able to discriminate between right and wrong and is respectable and trustworthy.

The concept of responsibility, like the concept of confidentiality, has moral, ethical and legal meaning. Its moral connotations are obvious, being that responsibility is ensuring that one does not harm another unduly with one's own actions. In the moral context it also can be summed up with phrases like 'Take care' or 'Do unto others as you would like to be treated yourself.' It is considered an adult attribute to be responsible. This for me means being able to rationalize one's thoughts and act appropriately on them. I believe that responsibility is a function of the mind and not of the heart. My reason for this is the fact that often we humans are irrational and irresponsible when emotive issues cloud our judgement, resulting in actions that can no longer be deemed as responsible. Moral responsibility is an attribute of character and all of us have it in varying degrees, whether it is to weaker, older or younger members of our communities, or simply paying the bills and making sure that there are clean clothes to wear. Put this type of responsibility in the context of the HIV-infected health care worker and the outcome may be very different. HIV is such an emotive issue that when bought up it can make us react to extremes. Yet many of us know that you cannot contract this disease casually and it is difficult to contract in comparison to other diseases such as tuberculosis or cholera which are far more infectious, spread airborne and from casual contact.

HIV is associated in most people's minds with blood. Procedures in the health care setting often result in bleeding and spattering. On first appearances it would seem that the health care setting is a dangerous place in terms of the possibility of contracting HIV. It is true that there are health care workers who have contracted HIV from their patients during clinical procedures, although the risk of this happening is comparable to other risks faced in the health care setting. Yet faced with a suspected HIV-infected colleague one may be tempted in the interests of public safety to report the suspect as a danger to patients. Initially this may seem justifiable, but on closer inspection we find that the risk of HIV transmission from an HIV-infected health care worker to patient does not warrant this action. Is this stance ethically questionable? There does exist a hypothetical risk that HIV could be transmitted from an HIV-infected health care worker to a patient if universal precautions are not observed during an exposure-prone procedure. And it is true that every nurse, midwife and health visitor has a responsibility to ensure the patient's safety at all times. So it might seem irresponsible to allow an HIV-infected health care worker to continue to work. Is our ethical responsibility of such magnitude as not to allow an even hypothetical risk?

The Department of Health have said that it is every health care worker's responsibility to be tested if they believe that they have been exposed under any circumstances to HIV. Such a policy throws the emphasis of testing onto the individual, appealing to one's moral responsibility whilst stressing that the responsibility is a professional one to ensure the safety of patients. It seems even a hypothetical risk is too big for this profession.

I do not believe in taking irresponsible risks, but such a policy supposedly in the interests of patients does not work. In the absence of mandatory testing, the responsibility to be tested rests with the individual. Any individual who has a test and tests positive is not allowed by the Department of Health to carry out exposure-prone procedures. Any health care worker considering the test may be put off by the possibility of being restricted in their work practices or even losing their career entirely. Many more health care workers who are practising must be ignorant of their status and have not as yet infected anyone. This would suggest that the risk is extremely small, even during exposure-prone procedures. Mandatory testing could be construed as being discriminatory and counter productive to the aims of the Department of Health and UKCC guidelines, which require people to come forward voluntarily and be tested. Discrimination against those who test HIV-positive can serve as a reason not to be tested in the first place. For those who are infected and unaware of their status, this may have ramifications for their own personal health in the future.

I do not believe that in the interests of ensuring personal safety one can rely on not allowing those who are infected with HIV to practice exposure-prone procedures. It is every health care worker's responsibility to ensure the safety of patients, which means we all need to take appropriate measures. That means it is *every* health care worker's responsibility to carry out universal precautions regardless of HIV status – known, suspected or otherwise.

This ideal carries over from the world of nursing into society. The ideal is that it is everybody's responsibility to protect themselves and others, although this was questioned in the summer of 1995. A question from a delegate at the Liberty human rights convention in June 1995 stunned the panel, which for about thirty seconds was unable or unwilling to answer the question. The question was, is it the responsibility of known HIV-infected people to always have safe sex and is it a criminal offence to infect someone without them knowing or is it the responsibility of the individual to protect oneself?

Present in the room at the time was a producer of the BBC's *Public Eye* and she started putting together a programme to examine this very question to be screened later that summer. Her research has uncovered a stark difference of opinion within the HIV sector. Some believe it is the responsibility of the infected individual to protect others, whilst others believe that it is each individual's responsibility to protect oneself.

There are very strong arguments for both views, but I feel that any argument leaning towards the responsibility being that of the known infected person is not conducive to any long-term HIV-prevention strategy. Those who believe themselves to be uninfected may abrogate any responsibility to practise safer sex. There are probably many people who are ignorant of their HIV status, and giving out the message that the responsibility to prevent HIV transmission belongs solely to infected people who are aware what their HIV status is, could lead to people unknowingly transmitting the virus and not testing themselves. Of course I do feel that to knowingly infect another is morally wrong, but I do not feel that it is fair, ethically viable or even sensible to rely solely on those who are known to be infected to carry the responsibility of preventing transmission.

If the responsibility belongs to those who are infected not to infect anyone else then surely there is a responsibility for everyone who believes or suspects themselves to be infected under any circumstances to know the position of their own HIV status. It seems unfair to restrict this policy to only known HIV-infected persons, and in doing so is discriminatory. Taking this line also brings up an old debate and could result in calls for mandatory testing to be implemented, something the HIV sector have advocated against for years.

The argument that it is the responsibility of everyone to take measures to protect themselves is an argument that stands up better than restricting the responsibility to only known HIV-infected persons. HIV in the western world primarily affects gay men, and to look at the HIV sector you could be led to believe it affects only gay men. Any policy to make the responsibility that of known infected people could backfire in the face of those who have made moves to re-gay the disease. (This theory has been developed by Edward King in *Safety in Numbers*.) With calls for gay men to take responsibility for protecting others, the logical progression of this argument is that gay men will be held more responsible for spreading the HIV virus. To criminalize the known transmission of HIV to another person could potentially lead to debate on whether in the interests of society homosexuality should be criminalized. Have those who advocated re-gaying the disease shot themselves in the foot and provided the moralists on the right with ammunition to fire at the gay community? If the HIV sector is seen to side with what the right wing have already been saying for years it could be construed they were correct all along.

Logically it seems sensible for everyone to take the responsibility for protecting themselves. It would be foolhardy to rely on others to do that for us. That is why HIV should be seen as affecting everybody. To directly place the responsibility on known HIV-infected people is to take a moral standpoint, something we have been trying to dismantle. Morality in transmission is a dangerous road to go down and segregates from society those who are already infected. It discourages people from coming forward for testing, as they see the discrimination other people face. This is dangerous to an individual's health and potentially to the health of others.

The question of this responsibility raised the level of public concern and reservations within the health care profession about the safety of clinically practising HIV-infected health care workers made it necessary for the UKCC to formulate guidelines with regards to HIV to remind health care workers of their professional responsibility and duty to the safety of patients. The guidance states:

> The Code of Professional Conduct requires each registered nurse, midwife and health
> visitor to serve the interests of society, and above all to safeguard the interests of the

individual patients and clients. It indicates that each registered nurse, midwife and health visitor is accountable for his or her practice, and, in the exercise of professional accountability shall:

'Act always in such a way as to promote and safeguard the well being and interests of patients/clients' (UKCC 1991) and 'Ensure that no action or omission on his/her part or within his/her sphere of influence is detrimental to the condition or safety of patients/clients' (UKCC 1991).

'All practitioners pose a potential infection risk, and all must ensure that high standards of clinical practice are maintained. The promotion of these standards is an important task for in-service education staff. If a nurse, midwife or health visitor is infected with HIV it is essential, however, that he or she take appropriate precautions to eliminate any possibility of blood or body fluid contamination to a patient. This necessitates the use of well established appropriate precautions to prevent transmission of any infection to a patient.' (Department of Health 1994)

The above guidance is based on current research and the knowledge we have on the virus today and attempts to reflect the fact that the risk to patients is virtually nil, although it is pointed out to the reader that regardless of HIV status, 'All practitioners pose a potential infection risk.'

With the use of well established Universal Infection Control Precautions, the risk of HIV transmission is restricted to exposure-prone procedures. All practitioners, irrespective of their HIV status, should scrupulously practise these precautions which are as follows:

1. Apply good basic hygiene practices with regular hand washing.
2. Cover existing wounds or skin lesions with waterproof dressings.
3. Avoid exposure-prone procedures if suffering from chronic skin lesions on hands.
4. Avoid contamination of person by appropriate use of protective clothing.
5. Protect mucous membrane of eyes, mouth and nose from blood splashes.
6. Prevent puncture wounds, cuts and abrasions in the presence of blood.
7. Avoid sharps usage wherever possible.
8. Institute safe procedures for handling and disposal of needles and other sharps.
9. Institute approved procedures for sterilization and disinfection of instruments and equipment.
10. Clear up spillages of blood and other body fluids promptly and disinfect surfaces.
11. Institute a procedure for the safe disposal of contaminated waste. (EAGA, 1990)

EXPOSURE-PRONE PROCEDURES

The guidance that preceded the UKCC's revised guidance published March 1994 used the term 'invasive procedure' throughout the text. This terminology only served to cause confusion. By definition, an invasive procedure would constitute any breaches of the skin or epithelia by a sharp instrument (Department of Health 1994). But in practice what actually constituted an 'invasive procedure' was widely debated, not only by the profession as a whole but also by whoever was reading the guidance on an individual basis. At the extreme, washing someone could be considered invasive, e.g. invasion of body space. The UKCC tightened up their terminology and redefined 'invasive procedure' with the term 'exposure-prone procedure' They went on to define what they actually meant by this, and state in their March 1994 guidance:

> Exposure-prone procedures are those where there is a risk that injury to the worker may result in the exposure of the patient's open tissues to the blood of the worker. These procedures include those where the worker's gloved hands may be in contact with sharp instruments, needle tips or sharp tissues (spicules of bone or teeth) inside a patient's open body cavity, wound or confined anatomical space where the hands or fingertips may not be completely visible at all times. Such procedures must not be performed by a health care worker who is either HIV-positive or Hepatitis B e antigen positive. The working practices of each infected health care worker must be considered individually and when there is any doubt expert advice should be sought in the first instance from a specialist occupational health physician who may in turn wish to consult the UK Advisory Panel (The Panel) which was set up under the aegis of EAGA in 1991. (Department of Health, 1994)

The guidance continues that 'Procedures where the hands and fingertips of the worker are visible and outside the patient's body at all times, and internal examinations or procedures that do not require the use of sharp instruments, are not considered to be exposure prone provided routine infection control procedures are adhered to at all times' (Department of Health, 1994).

The Department of Health does not consider the clinical practice of a general nurse working on a medical or surgical ward to involve exposure-prone procedures (Turnbull 1993); therefore HIV-positive nurses and students working in these environments could continue to work if they were asymptomatic. However, specialist environments such as accident and emergency, renal units, theatre and the delivery room, by the nature of work engaged in, involve procedures classified as exposure-prone. Therefore an HIV status would be seen to be incompatible with a continuation of unaltered clinical practice in these areas. If practice was modified, i.e. entailed abstention from exposure-prone procedures, a health care worker could continue to practice, although this does lead to questions with regard to confidentiality.

There has been much research to support the argument that health care workers pose no risk to patients when universal precautions are observed, yet over half the people in a survey carried out in the United States said they would no longer seek medical attention from a health care worker if they knew the worker was infected (Wicher, 1993).

> This statistic demonstrates an almost irrational fear on the part of the public, since the chance of actual transmission from health care worker to client is minimal. Over 10 years of epidemiological studies of HIV-infected health care workers who performed highly invasive procedures have indicated that no transmissions have occurred. Despite the laws and recommendations for employability of infected workers, there still exists widespread discrimination against individuals infected with HIV.

THE DILEMMA

The concern about HIV-infected health care workers practising might appear irrational and unfounded. Nevertheless the concern and fear does exist. The Department of Health are not in an enviable position. Despite their guidelines written to 'protect' the patient from potentially HIV-infected health care workers, and attempts to quell public panic, it is not under control. The social stigma of HIV makes it difficult not to discriminate against the health care worker, particularly when many of society's prejudices are reflected in the health care setting. To be forced to admit that all HIV-infected health care workers cannot be identified, has serious repercussions concerning trust and the profession's status in society. So the real question is 'How detrimental to patients are HIV-infected health care workers?'

The information and research that has been carried out into the possibility of HIV transmission from health care worker to patient suggests that there is virtually no risk to the patient when universal precautions are strictly adhered to. Yet the opinion of many is that HIV-infected health care workers pose a 'high risk' to patients. The Department of Health and the UKCC have tried to balance this risk whilst protecting the rights of health care workers, in the full knowledge that the risk is minuscule. The UKCC and Department of Health have taken prompt action in order to avoid risk, rather than waiting for a crisis to occur.

References

Department of Health (1994) *AIDS/HIV-Infected Health Care Workers: Guidance on the Management of Infected Health Care Workers*. London: DoH.

EAGA (1990) *Guidance for Clinical Health Care Workers: Protection Against Infection with HIV and Hepatitis Virus – Recommendations of the Expert Advisory Group on AIDS*. London: HMSO.

Hart, S. (1993) *Nursing Standard, HIV and Health Care Workers* (Part 1). London: Scutari Press.

King, E. (1993) *Safety in Numbers*. London: Cassell.

UKCC (1991) *Code of Professional Conduct*. London: UK Central Council for Nursing and Midwifery.

UKCC (1984) *Annual Report 1983–1984*. London: UKCC.

Wicher, C.P. (1993) AIDS/HIV: the dilemma of the health care worker. *AAOHN Journal*, June, 282–8.

CHAPTER 3

Risk and related issues

I note your bold statement that HIV cannot be transmitted through food. At a time when the specialists admit that there is so much that still baffles them about this dreadful scourge, I am amazed that you feel able to feel so certain.
Michael Cole, Director of Public Affairs, Harrods

This chapter has two parts. The first deals with the risk of transmitting the virus from health care worker to patient. It includes details of the David Acer case, the Florida dentist who is reported to have infected five of his patients. This case poses some interesting issues. The second part deals with the transmission of HIV from patient to health care worker. (I would also like to acknowledge Sue Morris's contribution to this chapter.)

TRANSMISSION OF HIV FROM HEALTH CARE WORKER TO PATIENT

The British Medical Association states that there is not one positively recorded case of HIV being transmitted by a health care worker to a patient during clinical procedure to date. It goes on to state that it would be extremely difficult for HIV to be transmitted to patients because:

- HIV almost certainly cannot pass through unbroken skin.
- HIV could only be transmitted if the health care worker's blood or other infectious body fluid entered the patient's body.
- Another virus, Hepatitis B, which is much more infectious than HIV, has been transmitted to patients only in isolated episodes involving only a few infected health care workers.
- Health Care Workers routinely take precautions to prevent infections being routinely transmitted from themselves to their patients.

The British Medical Association (1989) continue that 'There is however, an extremely small hypothetical risk that a patient could become infected with HIV if a health care worker were accidentally injured during a surgical procedure and if his or her blood entered the patient's body'.

We can make an estimate of the risk of HIV transmission during exposure-prone procedures based on our experience with Hepatitis B. HIV is of relatively low infectivity. Blood from an HIV-positive individual contains only 10 to the power of 4 virus particles and as much as 100μl of blood is necessary to transmit infection. Blood from a high-risk Hepatitis B carrier carries 10 to the power of 13 particles per ml and only 0.04μl of blood is necessary for transfer of infection.

Research into Hepatitis B transmission indicates that Hepatitis B is at least 100 times more infectious than HIV and probably ten times more common in health professionals (USA National Commission on AIDS, 1992). This would appear to be relatively high, except that the research was undertaken in operating theatres, and some procedures were cited as carrying higher risks than others. 'Experience with hepatitis B suggests that the risk of HIV transmission from a health care worker infected with HIV to a patient will be greatest during major surgical procedures' (*CDR Review*, 1994). In order to reflect the actual risk to patients during an exposure-prone procedure, research into injuries during these procedures is a necessity before the equation between infected health care workers and exposure-prone procedures can be made.

For the transmission of HIV from health care worker to patient to occur, the infected health care worker would have to sustain an injury and bleed into a patient's wound, or after sustaining an injury during an invasive procedure, have the sharp object causing the injury then recontact the patient's open wound or otherwise non-intact skin, resulting in the patient's exposure to the health care worker's blood (USA National Commission on AIDS 1992). Therefore HIV-infected health care workers must not carry out exposure-prone procedures, that is, 'procedures where there is a risk that injury to the health care worker may result in the exposure of the patient's tissues to the blood of the worker. This includes procedures where the workers gloved hands may be in contact with sharp instruments, needle tips or sharp tissues inside a patients open tissues, where the hands or fingertips may not be completely visible at all times' (Department of Health 1994).

The Department of Health's guidelines on HIV-infected health care workers are based upon the belief that 'general infection control measures are followed scrupulously' (Department of Health 1994). To observe universal precautions, health care workers protect themselves and their patients with barrier devices when anticipating contact with blood and body fluids. Barrier equipment for universal precautions includes protective gowns, latex and vinyl gloves, disposable face masks, and protective eye wear. Though it must be pointed out that there are appropriate times depending on the type of procedure and the amount of blood and spattering expected. For example, one would not wear a protective gown, face mask and eye wear to take samples of someone's blood, but would be expected to use protective clothing in the operating theatre during major surgery. This is because the highest risk of HIV transmission is thought to occur during major surgical procedures.

Whilst it is hoped that universal precautions are exercised at all times, infection control specialists are only too well aware that nurses are reluctant to adopt them. Allergies to latex, reduction in dexterity and peer pressure (*Nursing Times*, 1993) are but a few of the excuses made. There are also risks involved when a health care worker practises with exudative lesions and has inappropriately continued to practise, although no HIV transmissions have occurred this way as a result.

It is unlikely that a patient would know if they had been put at risk unless they were told.

This usually does not occur unless the health care worker discovers they are HIV-positive at a later date. In all the 'look-back' exercises that have been conducted, not a single patient has been found to be HIV-positive (*Digest*, 1993). It must also be remembered that this exercise does not take into consideration that a positive result may have been the result of exposure to infection in the patient's personal life, and not from the health care worker (Oakley *et al.* 1992).

Although unpleasant and often resulting in the identification of the worker concerned, look-back exercises provide us with about the best data as to the risks of transmission from a health care worker to a patient. This data is invaluable when it comes to assessing risks that may be involved during exposure-prone procedures. If an HIV-infected health care worker is known to have carried out exposure-prone procedures then it is quite possible a look-back exercise will occur. There are those who would argue that this is very costly. In the case of an HIV-infected London dentist the look-back exercise cost £100,000. Which budget this was going to come from was unknown at the time of writing, although it is possible it may come from the HIV budget. Some may argue that since no look-back exercise has ever revealed that an HIV-infected health care worker has been known to infect a patient it does not warrant the huge cost it takes to carry out such an exercise. I am inclined to disagree. For the time being it would be sensible to continue look-back exercises in the interests of patient safety and the accumulation of risk data. Any decisions to change policy would have to be based on this data. The number of patients world-wide who are known to have undergone exposure-prone procedures, been notified and subsequently tested is still too small to be 100 per cent confident that the risk of HIV transmission is negligible (*CDR Review* 1994). Much of the confusion surrounding the issue of when to test has been as a result of the limited data concerning actual transmission risks within the health care setting. Little research has been done to quantify the risks in any health care setting, which presents problems for the Department of Health when revising their guidelines (Skinner 1994). Without the data, risks remain 'potential' rather than 'actual'. The data on transmission risk of HIV during exposure-prone procedures at present is insufficient to provide a better estimation of risk (*CDR Review*, 1994).

DAVID ACER, FLORIDA DENTIST

The case of the Florida dentist David Acer who was reported to have infected five of his patients is well known. Mention HIV-infected health care workers to the average person on the street and he or she may well remind you of the case. The David Acer case throws up some very interesting points and we will look at the case in some detail.

David Acer died aged forty on 3 September 1990. He had been in general dentistry practice since 1980 and prior to that was in the military. Acer was bisexual and had a history of Hepatitis B going back several years. In 1986 he was diagnosed as being HIV-positive. He was shocked at this and although being told that his immune system was intact, developed Karposi Sarcoma, an AIDS-related skin cancer later the next year, for which he received chemotherapy. He also had an episode of presumptive PCP, an AIDS-related pneumonia (*AIDS Alert*, 1991a).

When patients called his office they were told that he had cancer although he had heard that several people knew that he had AIDS (*AIDS Alert*, 1991a). He told a social worker that it might be wrong for him to continue working without revealing his HIV status. According to medical reports he said 'Ethically and morally, I think I should not continue with my work without telling anybody' (*AIDS Alert*, 1991b). Despite his conscience, fears that public knowledge of his HIV status would hurt the scale of his dental practice, which at the time was thriving, prevented him from telling friends and staff about his infection. He planned to sell his practice before he was too weak to continue working.

A review of Acer's medical records depicts a man who kept his bisexuality and his HIV infection a closely guarded secret. He appeared to give conflicting information to the various people who treated him and interviewed him. Much of the information in his medical records is sketchy, so the story contains some inconsistencies that cannot be explained. He sought medical care under the name of David Johnson (Johnson was Acer's middle name). On diagnosis of Karposi's Sarcoma he confessed that his name was David Acer and that he was by profession a dentist. Acer said that hiding his diagnosis was 'lonely and isolating'.

On 29 March 1990 Acer was interviewed in connection with the possible transmission of HIV to one of his patients, Kimberly Bergalis, the first person found to be infected. He told the CDC investigator who interviewed him that after discovering he was HIV-positive he always wore gloves and a mask for each patient and had stopped using alcohol as a disinfectant. However, interviews with staff suggest that this was not the case. Acer signed a consent form to have his blood taken for a polymerase chain reaction test and other experimental studies, although he was not completely co-operative. The results of the epidemiological and laboratory investigations indicated that Bergalis became infected with HIV while receiving care from Acer. DNA sequence analysis showed her strain of HIV to have a high degree of similarity to that of her dentist. The same is true of tests carried out on four of his other patients. We can safely say that Acer's infected patients carried very similar strains of HIV and it is likely that the infection came from him. The question is, how?

It was debated whether Acer had infected his patients through negligence or if he infected them intentionally, as a revenge on society. This provided a heyday for the world press. Given that HIV is largely contracted by those with certain sexual and drug use behaviours, the amount of media attention devoted to health care workers with the disease is staggering. In July 1991 both *Time* and *Newsweek* featured articles on the topic. *Newsweek*'s cover portrayed a gaunt and obviously very ill family practitioner from Minneapolis. Inside, his photograph was juxtaposed with a deathbed image of Kimberly Bergalis, a strong visual suggestion that people who go to doctors, dentists or hospitals are risking their lives (Fox, 1991).

The probable route of transmission in the case of David Acer was a lapse of universal precautions. We know from interviews with his staff that there were discrepancies in accounts of the use of universal precautions and how they were carried out. On 31 August 1990, David Acer was transferred from the hospital where he was a patient with chest pain to a hospice. That same day he wrote an open letter that was published in a local newspaper. He told his former patients that it was unlikely that he was responsible for the transmission of HIV because he 'strictly adhered' to universal precautions. He said in his letter, 'I am writing this letter because I am concerned that with the recent news regarding me in the local media, you are afraid that you may have been infected with the disease commonly known as AIDS . . . I want to reassure you that it is unlikely you have been infected with the disease from me and I urge you to seek the free testing and counseling that is available from your local health department'. (*AIDS Alert*, 1991b)

Three days later David Acer died, aged forty.

Kimberly Bergalis became a symbol for an outraged nation. She had said she was a virgin, and therefore unlikely to contract HIV. She campaigned to Congress to introduce mandatory testing for health care workers. In her words, during a televised plea:

'I have done nothing wrong, yet I am being made to suffer like this. My life has been taken away. Please enact legislation so that no other patient or health care provider will have to go through the hell that I have.' (*Midwinter*, 1994)

Just before her death, insurance companies were forced to pay her and two others who eventually died, over £6,000,000 in compensation (*Midwinter*, 1994). After Kimberly and the others had died investigators were employed by the insurance companies to delve into the private lives of Acer's patients and the information they dug up shocked America. It was reported like this:

'The American public couldn't quite believe what it was seeing. As the top-rated show *Sixty Minutes* was broadcast on CBS last week, the television channel's switchboard was immediately jammed with calls from coast to coast.

In the progamme, a young woman was confessing on video to a sexual encounter with a boyfriend. Ordinarily, in America, such admissions are hardly shocking. But what made this so extraordinary is that the woman was Kimberly Bergalis, the Florida student who had died of AIDS three years ago and who, right up until her death, maintained that she was a virgin with an unblemished sexual past.' (*Midwinter*, 1994)

In reporting the 'tragedy' of Acer's infected patients, all had claimed they were either virgins or had never involved themselves in any high risk activity. Therefore, dentist-to-patient transmission of the virus looked most likely (*Midwinter*, 1994). But the investigations carried out by the insurance companies showed that the other 'victims' also had pasts, from claims of prostitutes, to extramarital affairs, to dealing crack for sex and intravenous drug use (*Midwinter*, 1994). It remains to be seen whether in the future the insurance companies will try to recoup the money. One could be cynical and suggest that such a move would be just to ensure that it was more difficult for people to claim damages. Kimberly Bergalis's dramatic confession cannot be cited as the key element in this affair. Although the confession throws a slight shadow of doubt on the whole subject, it must be remembered that DNA sequencing proved that the strains of HIV carried by the patients were virtually the same as Acer's.

In conclusion, it is likely that David Acer infected five of his patients. As far as the route of transmission is concerned we may never know how it happened.

TRANSMISSION OF HIV FROM PATIENT TO HEALTH CARE WORKER

The risk of transmission of the HIV virus from patient to health care worker is clearer than from health care worker to patient. The first case of HIV being transmitted in this way was reported in 1994 (*CDR Review*, 1994). By May 1995, 214 cases of occupationally acquired infection were reported (Department of Health, 1995).

Despite the risk being low, it is obvious that the health care worker is at more risk from his or her patient than the other way around. Health care workers should always take appropriate precautions to protect themselves. We can categorize the risk of exposure to blood and suggest protective measures to prevent cross contamination thus:

> If contact of a health care worker with blood is probable and there is potential for uncontrolled bleeding or spattering, i.e., major surgical, gynecological and obstetrical procedures, a full range of protective clothing should be available. When spattering is unlikely, i.e., intra-arterial punctures, insertion of intravenous/intra-arterial lines, gloves should be worn and protective eye wear should be available. Where personal contact is unlikely, ie., administration of intra-muscular, intra-dermal or subcutaneous injections, gloves should be available. (EAGA, 1990)

It is good practice to apply these precautions to all patients regardless of known HIV status, as patients may be unaware of their own situation.

Occupational exposure to the virus may take the form of a percutaneous or muco-cutaneous exposure. A percutaneous exposure is one in which the skin is cut or penetrated by a needle or other sharp object (e.g., scapel blade, trocar, tooth, bone spicule) (*CDR Review*, 1993). A mucocutaneous exposure is one which involves the eye(s), inside of the nose or mouth, or an area of non-intact skin of the person exposed (*CDR Review*, 1993). The chance that a single percutaneous exposure will result in infection is about 0.3 per cent. The risk of infection after a mucocutaneous exposure is much lower, probably less than 0.1 per cent (Public Health Laboratory Service, 1993).

Even if a health care worker is exposed to an infected patient's blood or other body fluids, the risk of the worker becoming infected with HIV is very low. Body fluids include blood products, semen, vaginal secretions, cerebrospinal fluid, synovial fluid, pleural fluid, peritoneal fluid, pericardial fluid, and amniotic fluid. Countries with well developed health services have incorporated procedures for monitoring workplace exposure to HIV within established systems for reporting workplace injuries. Such surveillance allows the size of the problem and degree of risk to be quantified, and potentially hazardous working practices and procedures may be identified. For the purposes of national surveillance, a significant HIV exposure is defined as one in which a health care worker sustains either:

1. A percutaneous exposure to blood or body fluids from a source known or found to be HIV infected; or
2. A percutaneous or mucocutaneous exposure to laboratory fluid known to contain live virus; or
3. A mucocutaneous exposure to blood from a source known or found to be HIV-infected.

It is important that good practice for the management of significant exposure incidents is followed, which results in useful data that can be used in the future. The surveillance system has evolved only as more information about the risks of occupational exposure has become available, and ultimately this information can be used to promote a safer environment.

The data accumulated by the surveillance centres suggests that the main hazard to health care workers is percutaneous exposure to HIV-infected blood, particularly exposure which involves fresh blood and hollow needles (*CDR Review*, 1993). Conversely, the interpersonal transmission of AIDS via scalpels, suture needles, scissors, or bone-invasive tools remains to be well documented anywhere (Jagger *et al.*, 1991). Of the documented seroconversions following occupational exposure described in sufficient detail to allow evaluation, three-quarters resulted from occupational exposure with contaminated hollow-bore needles (*CDR Review*, 1993).

As most occupational exposures occur with hollow-bore needles contaminated with HIV-infected blood, great care obviously should be taken when handling them. Gloves are no protection from needle stick injuries, although glove material of any type will reduce the amount of contamination. This is because during punctures, the glove itself acts as a sheath, stripping some of the blood from the needle's exterior, and thus may well reduce the amount of blood transferred. The occupationally acquired infections reported to the Communicable Diseases Surveillance Centre found that three out of four UK health care workers in whom seroconversion was documented were known to have been wearing gloves at the time of exposure in accordance with current guidance (*CDR Review*, 1993). Other factors must also be taken into consideration that may influence the degree of risk of seroconversion, but are difficult to quantify. These include the stage of HIV disease and the viral load of the 'source patient' and the immunologic competence of the individual who is injured. The prevalence of HIV infection is also an important consideration in assessing the cumulative risk to health care workers over time (USA National Commission on AIDS 1992).

PREVENTING NEEDLE STICK INJURIES

Needle stick injuries are the most common form of occupational exposure in the health care setting, although there is only a 0.5 per cent risk of transmission from a needle containing contaminated blood. The BMA reported in a survey that out of 326 needle stick injuries 113 occurred with disposable syringes and 86 of those took place after the needle had been used. In seven cases the cap fell off the needle, in 13 cases the cap was pierced and in 32 cases the practitioner missed the sheath whilst attempting to re-sheath the needle (Anderson *et al.*, 1991).

The use of needles in the health care setting is a necessary way of administering medication to patients and the Department of Health have issued guidelines on the use of needles. The guidance states, 'Needles that have to be removed from syringes and lines must be dealt with safely. Needle forceps or other suitable aids or devices should be readily available. Up to 40 per cent of self-inoculation accidents have been reported to occur while re-sheathing needles: therefore this must not be done unless there is a safe means available at the point where the work is being conducted' (Advisory Committee on Dangerous Pathogens, 1990).

The high incidence rate of occupational accidents to do with re-sheathing needles prompted the United States Centers for Disease Control to opt for a non-sheathing technique for health care workers disposing of needles. Although there is little evidence for the efficacy of the practice, these recommendations were based on the assumption that avoiding re-sheathing should decrease the number of needle stick injuries.

Throughout this book I have advocated the use of universal precautions in the workplace to minimize the risk of HIV transmission from a health care worker to patient, but are universal precautions sufficient enough to prevent needle stick injuries, the most common cause of occupational exposure to HIV?

There is a growing body of evidence to suggest that universal precautions alone are not sufficient to reduce the risk of needle stick injuries and there is growing concern that reliance on universal precautions to prevent needle stick injuries is delaying a transition to safer needle designs. In time we will be able to measure that delay by the number of health care workers who have contracted fatal and preventable disease (Jagger *et al.*, 1991). In a 1994 article in *AIDS Alert* it was reported that more than one out of every two health care workers re-sheathed needles, and at least one of every four reported at least one percutaneous injury (*AIDS Alert*, 1994). That is an alarming percentage of occupational exposures, and even if the risk of HIV transmission is minuscule the fact remains that there are many more cases of HIV transmission from patient to health care worker than the other way around. Although universal precautions are sufficient enough to protect the patient from the HIV-infected health care worker, they are not enough to protect the health care worker entirely from occupational exposure to the virus.

Needle stick injuries happen for a variety of reasons beyond the practice of re-sheathing. A significant number happen during resuscitative procedures. Resuscitation is often frantic and virtually an organized chaos when it is a very possible occasion for an accidental needle stick injury to occur. This can only be described as an occupational hazard, just as a burning roof falling on a fireman or a policeman shot during a bank raid could be described as occupational hazards. The risk associated with percutaneous exposures to symptomatic HIV-positive patients is comparable to other risks that health care workers have faced knowingly and have accepted in the recent past (Owens and Nease 1992). I would say that there are two different categories of needle stick injury. Those that occur as an occupational hazard and that are unavoidable and those that happen due to confusion over disposal practices and are therefore avoidable.

If one is involved personally in a needle stick injury it can be a very traumatic time indeed. Health care workers infected with HIV in the workplace are portrayed by the British tabloid press as being innocent victims of the epidemic, which is discussed in more detail in chapter six. It should be understood that the health care worker goes through the same emotional process as anyone else who believes that they may have been infected. Pauline Dobson is a clinical nurse consultant in New South Wales, Australia. She wrote a small diary on the events that followed exposure and it was published in the *British Medical Journal* in 1992. I have reproduced it here as it gives us a very good insight into how a health care worker may feel after being exposed.

Diary of a needle stick injury
By Pauline Dobson

Earlier this year I suffered a needle stick injury during a difficult central line procedure. The patient was terminally ill with AIDS and fortunately was unaware of my injury. After assessment by the immunologist the decision was made that the injury was high risk and that treatment with Zidovudine should be considered. Whenever a colleague sustained a needle stick injury in the past I had decided that I would take Zidovudine if it happened to me. I took my first dose and tried to assimilate all that was going on around me.

Whenever I am faced with a stressful event I cope by trying to minimize and deny it. With everyone fussing around me it was impossible to minimize the experience but I kept trying.

People who knew of the exposure would ask, 'Are you all right?' with a knowing look. This concern became unbearable. It kept reminding me of what had happened when I was desperately trying to forget.

Sometimes I wonder whether the reactions of those around me were based on the concern for themselves and not just for me. 'There but for the grace of God go I'. This is understandable, no one wants to be reminded of their vulnerability when they work with patients with AIDS. As a nurse's consultant I felt that I was expected to be a role model, and this weighed heavily on me. I presented an exterior that was outwardly cool and calm but inside I was suffering immense turmoil. I was terribly disappointed with my reaction. I wanted to be able to handle it better. I have witnessed many doctors' and nurses' reactions to occupational exposure. Yet those who reacted with near paranoia I looked on as weak and foolish. I thought, 'If you can't stand the heat get out of the kitchen'. I can now empathize with some of their feelings of insecurity and fear.

One of my greatest problems was telling my husband. He had always been supportive of my desire to work with people with HIV infection and AIDS but has remained concerned about the risk of contracting HIV. I wished I could avoid telling him until after my final test. But I knew that if I had become infected I would need to protect him. I couldn't justify the use of condoms without an explanation. He coped amazingly well and I was immediately relieved.

As the days passed I become nauseous and sleepy from the treatment. I wondered how I was going to cope with another six weeks. I have a busy schedule and at times I found it impossible to take Zidovudine four hourly. I missed quite a few doses. One of the difficult things was that every four hours I was reminded that I had a needle stick exposure. After five days I decided to stop the treatment.

I give lectures to nurses and the question of needle stick injuries always arises. It is hard to present the facts and remain detached when the issue is so clouded in personal emotions. But I worked hard to separate my experience from my duties. I read journal articles to keep up with the rapidly changing field. I had to present an article on the acute seroconversion illness at a journal club meeting. Among the presentations of seroconversion there were several cases of palatal ulcers. One week later I developed ulcers. My husband was aware of this but not of the article and at mealtimes he watched my face contorted with pain and I had to constantly reassure him that this was not part of HIV infection. Deep down I was trying to reassure myself that the ulcers were stress induced and not related to seroconversion. My husband quizzed me every time I sneezed, and I found this difficult to cope with.

The crunch came during the sixth week after the injury. I was watching the television news and there was a report about seroconversion in another health care worker in New South Wales. My husband started to express his fears. I exploded. I had enough trouble trying to deal with my own feelings and fears without the extra burden of his. That night I received a telephone call from a friend who had watched the news and wanted to know whether I was the health care worker. She was concerned. I reassured her. I couldn't believe it. Here I was going through all this personal trauma and I had to support everyone around me. I felt for the person who was reported on the news. It had been easy to deny that it could happen to me before this. But hearing about the seroconversion six weeks after my own exposure was devastating.

Throughout the whole ordeal I received tremendous support from the immunologist. He was always there at a minute's notice. I tried not to convey my fears of becoming infected and how vulnerable I felt. I did not want him to think that I was not coping. My first test at seven weeks gave negative results. The immunologist seemed just as thrilled at the result as I was. It raised my spirits enormously. All the odds were in my favour: most seroconversions from exposures occur in the first six weeks.

This experience has altered so many of my attitudes, about my colleagues, my patients, my family, and myself. I will never be the same person. This is not a depressing thought. I certainly understand much more about what my patients got through waiting for test results. Most health care workers and health administrators do not understand the psychological consequences of a high risk exposure. I hope this story helps their understanding.

My final test at three months gave negative test results. The immunologist opened a bottle of wine to celebrate the news.

(This article is reproduced with the kind permission of the *British Medical Journal*.)

The story of Pauline Dobson illustrates the case of a health care worker occupationally exposed in the course of duty. I can fully identify with her feelings when she was waiting for the test results. I think the case also shows that needle stick injuries can also happen as the result of a genuinely hazardous situation as well as the practice of re-sheathing needles. I do not believe that universal precautions would have been enough to protect the worker in this situation and although it may sound a bit glib, it amounts to an accident. As I have already said, the risks that health care workers face are comparable to other risks that they face in the workplace. However, we can make an effort to keep this risk a small as possible.

In the first instance health care workers should feel able to report incidents involving sharp instruments. Linda Martin, PhD, director of the National Institute of Occupational Safety and Health's HIV activities at the federal Centers for Disease Control and Prevention in Atlanta, was quoted as saying that all too often health care workers were reluctant to report their needle stick injuries out of fear of losing their jobs (*AIDS Alert*, 1994a).

Once again we find health care workers too frightened to talk about the possibility of being infected with HIV to their occupational health departments for fear of losing their jobs. In the case of needle stick injuries questions may be raised about the competency of a health care worker. Whilst I believe that it is important that as much detail as possible should be collected about how a sharps accident has happened, it should be remembered that needle stick injuries also happen purely as accidents and not always as a result of bad clinical practice.

An article published by the *Lancet* (1994) suggested that there is a greater risk of injuries to people working night shifts. Health care is a twenty-four hour job and the hours of a health care worker do not fit the frame of the normal working day of between 0700 and 1800. The *Lancet* reported that since the 1940s, the decrease in performance associated with night work has been repeatedly documented. They cite examples such as errors in meter readings, slowness in connecting telephone calls, longer reaction times, and reduced alertness. It is safe to say that health care workers would be at more risk at night from a needle stick injury.

Despite the advice given on preventing needle stick injuries they are going to occur, so what should be done when a needle stick injury happens? In the first instance one should:

1. Encourage the injection site to bleed freely for a few minutes.
2. Clean the area with warm, soapy water and dry.
3. Inform the appropriate line manager of the injury.

As soon as the accident happens one should start applying this procedure. Some health care officials suggest that cleansing with an antiseptic soap may also help; although it may not reduce the risk of HIV infection, it might help to eliminate the development of other microbacterial problems not associated with the AIDS virus. (*AIDS Alert*, 1989)

In terms of medical assistance after a needle stick injury, Zidovudine may be offered as prophylactic therapy after exposure. Zidovudine is also known as Retrovir or more commonly AZT. It is manufactured by Glaxo Wellcome. Its effectiveness in terms of pro-phylactic treatment after occupational exposure is not very well documented and because the number of people who seroconvert after occupational exposure to HIV is so small (0.33 per cent after a percutaneous exposure) it is difficult even to estimate its usefulness. There do not appear to be any firm guidelines on its usage. The CDC take a non-committal approach. I personally cannot advocate whether or not one should take Zidovudine after a needle stick injury, although I do believe that health care workers should be offered the choice of taking it in full knowledge of any side effects and knowing that this treatment after exposure is no guarantee that it will work.

Health care officials agree that the most important line of action one should take after having had a needle stick injury is to tell one's employer (*AIDS Alert*, 1989). Some might think that this leaves the health care worker in the situation of deciding themselves if an accident is serious enough to be reported. Eddie Hedrick, manager of the infection control department in staff services at the University of Missouri Hospital in Columbia, is reported to have said that 'We don't want [the injured workers] to determine if medical attention is needed, we want them, if they get a needle puncture, to come down to employee health, and we'll determine for them if they need medical attention' (*AIDS Alert*, 1989). Once again we see the need for constructive efforts ·to maintain some sort of safe environment for health care workers in which they can come forward and report any accident. Such trust is vital to the success of any policy or guidance on the subject on the management of HIV-infected health care workers. I believe one way of doing this would be to involve health care workers and encourage their input into good needle stick prevention programmes. Health care workers could then talk about devices or procedures that they may find difficult to carry out whilst scrupulously employing universal precautions.

It needs to be emphasized to health care workers on a regular basis how they should use and dispose of sharps. Notices alerting health care workers to the risk of HIV and indeed much more virulent blood-borne viruses should be placed where health care workers are going to see them regularly. Sharps bins should be plentiful and placed as near as possible to wherever sharps are in usage. They should never be more than two thirds full.

Health care workers are at more risk from HIV-infected patients than the other way around. The risk to patients from infected health care workers is virtually nil when universal precautions are carried out scrupulously. All practitioners and patients pose a potential infection risk, and these precautions apply to everybody, not only known infected persons. One is more likely to die from smoking or a car accident than being infected by an HIV-infected health care worker or indeed occupationally infected by a patient.

Safe Practising!

References

Advisory Committee on Dangerous Pathogens (1990) *HIV: The Causative Agents of AIDS and Related Conditions*. Second revision of guidelines. London: HMSO.

AIDS Alert (1989) Needle stick injuries: what should be done when they occur (AIDS guide for health care workers). **4** (4), S3.

AIDS Alert (1991a) CDC notes from interview with David Acer. (Centres for Disease Control investigation of dentist who transmitted AIDS) (special issue on David Acer case). **6** (7), 124.

AIDS Alert (1991b) Florida dentist troubled about keeping his HIV status secret (special issue on David Acer case). **6** (7), 130.

AIDS Alert (1994a) Good needle stick prevention programs encourage employee input. **9** (4), S1.

AIDS Alert, (1994b), CDC suspicions confirmed: precautions not universal. **9** (6), 80.

Anderson, D. C, Blower, A. L, Packer, J. M. V and Gnguli, L. A. (1991) Preventing needle stick injuries. *British Medical Association*, **302** (6779), 769.

British Medical Association (1989) Parliamentary Fact Sheet. Healthcare workers infected with HIV. London: BMA Foundation for Aids.

CDR Review (1993) Health care workers and HIV: Surveillance of occupationally acquired infection in the United Kingdom. **3** (11), 8 October.

CDR Review (1994) Outcome of an exercise to notify patients treated by an obstetrician/gynaecologist infected with HIV–1. **4** (11), 14 October.

Cole, M., Director of Public Affairs, Harrods. Correspondence written to Ms Vannessa Hardy at the National AIDS Trust.

Department of Health (1994) *AIDS/HIV Infected Health Care Workers: Guidance on the Management of HIV Infected Health Care Workers*. London: HMSO.

Digest (1993) Confusing and contradictory beliefs complicate debate. *Digest of Organizational Responses to AIDS/HIV*, **2** (3), May.

Dobson, Pauline (1992) Diary of a needle stick injury (nurse sticks self with needle during procedure on AIDS patient) (Personal view) (Column). *British Medical Journal*, **305** (6865), 1372.

EAGA (1990) *Recommendations of the UK Advisory Panel for health care workers infected with blood borne viruses. General counter infection control measures for the clinical setting.*

Fox, Christopher H. (1991) Hazardous health care? (transmission of AIDS). *Harvard Health Letter* **17** (1), 4.

Jagger, Janine, Pearson, Richard D., Wong, Edward S., Markowitz, Sheldon M. and Mcguire, Hunter Holmes (1991) Do universal precautions reduce needle stick injuries? (Includes reply) (Letter to the editor). *Journal of the American Medical Association*, **266** (3), 359.

Lancet (1994) Hazarding the night (greater risk of injury in people working night shifts). **344** (8930), 1099 (2).

Midwinter (1994) Death bed confession of the girl who got AIDS from dentist is dividing America. 26 June.

Nursing Times (1993) Prehiring HIV test invades privacy. **89** (23), 28 April.

Oakley, K., Gooch, C. and Cockcroft, A. (1992) Review of management of incidents involving exposure to blood in a London teaching hospital 1989–1991. *British Medical Journal*, **304**, 11 April.

Owens, Douglas K. and Nease, Robert F. (1992) Occupational exposure to human immunodeficiency virus hepatitis B virus: a comparative analysis of risk. **92** (5), 503.

Public Health Laboratory Service (1993) *Surveillance of occupational exposure to HIV: information for health care workers and their carers.*

Skinner, R. (1994) Look back studies needed. *Nursing Times*, **90** (18), 14 May.

USA National Commission on AIDS (1992) *Preventing HIV transmission in health care settings.*

CHAPTER 4

Rights and the HIV-positive health care worker

Liberal humanists and friends of the homosexual lobby have taken over policy in the Department of Health, emphasizing the rights of those infected with AIDS and HIV to the exclusion of their responsibilities, the precise opposite of Conservative principles.

(Conservative Family Campaign 1991)

Health care workers should have the same rights as any other free person in this country enjoys. All citizens of the United Kingdom, including people with HIV and AIDS, are accorded the following rights under international law:

- the right to liberty and security of person
- the right to privacy
- the right to freedom of movement
- the right to work
- the right to housing, food, social security, medical assistance and welfare
- the right to freedom from inhumane or degrading treatment
- the right to equal protection of the law and protection from discrimination
- the right to marry
- the right to found a family
- the right to education

There are three areas of human rights which especially need to be looked at in relation to the HIV-infected health care worker: the right to work, the right to privacy and the right to protection from discrimination.

THE RIGHT TO WORK

Every one under international law has the right to work, or at least that is the theory. Factors such as economic growth and therefore availability of work make this right difficult to achieve. There may always be more workers than jobs, particularly with the fast-growing information technology market making administration supposedly simpler, faster and cheaper. In the United Kingdom, those who do not or cannot work may receive state benefits to live on. This all adds up; to the yearly amounts of benefit paid, must be added administration costs and salaries for the civil servants who work to pay those who don't or can't earn for themselves because of their circumstances. People living with HIV may well stay healthy for many years, though often when employers find out an employee's HIV status they may be fired, retired, or signed off sick indefinitely. Is the state expected to pick up the tab? Can someone rely on the state to pay reasonable money to them if they are forced to leave their place of work? This dilemma is a catch twenty-two situation. If one is not sick enough then one will not receive benefits for invalidity or disability and may have to live on little more than £60 a week. If the HIV-infected health care worker, whom the state has paid a fortune to train, is scrapheaped with the possibility of never practising again, a valuable social commodity is wasted.

Considering the minuscule risks involved when an HIV-infected health care worker continues to practise, there is little to stop them from practising so long as exposure-prone procedures are not carried out and universal precautions are observed. This is the case for the known infected health care worker. Though there must be many HIV-infected health care workers practising who are ignorant of their status, as far as we know there have been no transmissions occurring this way in Britain to date. I believe therefore that to stop HIV-infected health care workers from working is unnecessary in the light of current transmission risk data. 'Every one has the right to the opportunity to gain his living by work which he freely chooses or accepts' (Sieghart 1989). However, it does seem that as health care workers we waiver our rights over work as defined by the World Health Organisation and International law. The Declaration of the Rights of People with HIV and AIDS, of which the Royal College of Nursing is a signatory, states that people with HIV and AIDS have the right to work, and in respect of this right the signatories of the declaration believe that:

- No person should be barred from employment purely on the grounds of their having HIV, or having AIDS or an AIDS related condition;
- Employers should ensure that their terms and conditions of employment are such as to enable people with HIV, AIDS or an AIDS related condition to continue in this employment, and to do so in a healthy and safe working environment;
- Employers or their agents should not perform tests to detect the HIV status of current or prospective employees;
- In respect of the right to work, the right to privacy, and the right to protection from discrimination, there should be no obligation or requirement upon an individual to disclose to an employer their own HIV status, or the HIV status of another person. (Declaration)

Although the declaration is signed by, amongst others, the Royal College of Nursing, the National AIDS trust and the Terrence Higgins Trust, it is not recognized by the British government as an enforceable document. Although it is based on international law, the Declaration should be seen as no more than a set of standards in an ideal world.

Let us consider further each point made by the declaration on the rights to work. It is clear that the first point advises us that no one should be dismissed from employment purely on the grounds of their HIV status. 'The UN committee on Economics, Social and Cultural Rights, interpreting the provisions of the relevant International Covenant, has emphasized that an effective guarantee against arbitrary dismissal is an integral element of the right to work.' (Sieghart 1989). The reasons for any dismissal should be objectively relevant to the performance of the duties of employment. 'It follows that, if an applicant for a job were refused employment, or an employee were dismissed solely on the ground that he or she was – or suspected of being HIV-positive, this would constitute an interference with his or her right to work unless it could be established that the absence of infection was a bona fide and necessary occupational qualification, or that the infection would clearly and substantially affect job performance.' (Sieghart 1989).

Although someone may be HIV-infected, so long as they are healthy there is no reason why HIV should affect their job performance, although deteriorating health may be a factor that would affect any health care worker in terms of what is required of them for the job. The absence of HIV is not officially stated as being a necessary occupational qualification, indeed the Department of Health have openly stated that HIV-infected general nurses are welcome to practise. But in reality, any health care worker known to be HIV-infected prior to employment is likely to be refused on the grounds of health, depending on the attitude of the occupational health physician. If the absence of HIV were a necessary qualification for the employment of health care workers, this would mean the introduction of mandatory testing for health care workers, which many conclude is unethical and unworkable.

The Department of Health guidance on the management of HIV-infected health care workers operates on the assumption that if one believes themselves to have been exposed to HIV then they should seek medical advice and, if appropriate, diagnostic testing. It must be said that erosion of employment rights only serves to stop people from coming forward and being tested in the first place. All employers should be aware of the rights of their workers and visibly enforce the ethos of employment rights by allowing HIV-infected health care workers to continue working if healthy and not involved in exposure-prone procedures. Unfortunately I feel that in these days of radical change in the health service, many hospital managers may see an HIV-infected health care worker as more of a liability than an asset and one that should be dumped quickly to avoid damaging business. With evidence of this sort of attitude it is quite understandable that anyone who believes they may have been exposed to the virus may think twice about who they tell or having the test in the first place, making the guidelines on the management of HIV-infected health care workers even harder to enforce.

The second point raised by the declaration is that employers should ensure that people with HIV or AIDS are able to continue working and are able to do so in a safe environment. The Department of Health have tried to protect this right in their Guidance which states:

> Health care workers must also be assured that their status to rights as employees will be safeguarded so far as practicable. Employers must make every effort to arrange suitable alternative work and retraining opportunities, or where appropriate, early retirement, in accordance with good general principles of occupational health practice. (Department of Health, 1994).

Whether an HIV-infected health care worker can safely work in the hospital environment is very much dependent on the stage of their disease. Obviously if a health care worker was susceptible to infection because of immuno suppression and the type of working environment, the employer would be irresponsible to allow them to continue to work. This illustrates an occasion where one person's personal view of HIV and what being HIV-positive means in terms of health and risk to others is a factor in deciding one's fitness to work. It is vitally important that the occupational health department be aware of the fact that being HIV and healthy is not grounds for removal from the workplace, although it is its duty to monitor the health of the worker and if such a situation arises where the infected health care worker is in danger because of progression of the HIV virus, the authorities cannot guarantee a healthy environment for the worker.

The third and fourth points in the Declaration on the rights to work concern the testing employees and their obligation to tell employers of their HIV status. There are some major differences in this respect between the Declaration and the official documents of the UKCC and the Department of Health. The UKCC clearly state in their statement on HIV and AIDS that 'a nurse, midwife or health visitor who believes that she or he may have been exposed to infection with HIV, in whatever circumstances, should seek medical advice and diagnostic testing' (UKCC 1994). The Department of Health state in their document that 'health care workers who are infected with HIV must seek appropriate expert medical and also occupational health advice' (Department of Health 1994). In contrast, the Declaration states that 'there should be no obligation or requirement upon an individual to disclose to an employer their own HIV status'. The World Health Organization states in its guidelines on HIV and AIDS in the workplace that 'there should be no obligation for the employee to inform the employer regarding his or her HIV/AIDS status' (World Health Organization 1994). These are clearly differing stances when it comes to HIV-infected health care workers.

However, because of the theoretical potential risk of HIV transmission from an infected health care worker to a patient, and bearing in mind the UKCC's Code of Professional Conduct reminding us that as health care workers we are 'personally accountable' and should 'ensure that no action or omission on one's part, or within one's sphere of responsibility, is detrimental to the interests, condition or safety of patients and clients' (UKCC, 1991), it can be said that the Declaration of the Rights of People with HIV and AIDS does not apply to health care workers in respect of there being no obligation or requirement upon an individual to disclose to an employer their own HIV status.

Health care workers may need to stop practising any aspect of their work that involves exposure-prone procedures. But if the worker is not involved in exposure-prone procedures, and 'given knowledge of the means of transmission, there is no reason to dismiss or suspend such an employee on the grounds that they pose an unacceptable risk to patients' (UKCC, 1994).

If an employee must be stopped altogether from practising in an area where exposure-prone procedures are involved, efforts should be made to re-assign the worker to a safer area of practice whilst trying to maintain the salary and position of the worker. Re-assignment of the worker is the responsibility of the employer, as stated in the UKCC's statement on HIV and AIDS and in the Department of Health's Guidance.

The only criticism I have of the Department of Health guidance concerns the subject of early retirement. A specialist occupational health physician would ultimately have the final say as to whether or not one was fit to work. It should be noted that many still believe that to be HIV-positive is to be ill and many forget that one can be HIV-positive and healthy for many years. Other health care professionals' lack of HIV awareness can be detrimental to one's career, as can any possible prejudices or discriminatory views held by those making decisions that affect us. It should be the right of any health care worker to seek a second opinion if they do not agree with that of one specialist occupational health physician. On assessing the health of an HIV-infected health care worker the Department of Health states that 'all infected health care workers should receive regular care from a physician experienced in HIV'.

Although I feel that the UKCC and Department of Health have acted quickly to prevent any potential transmission occurring in this country of HIV from a health care worker to a patient, I do believe that they initially overreacted. Whilst there is no longer an obligation to inform on colleagues, there is a responsibility to seek appropriate advice and possibly diagnostic testing if one believes oneself to have been exposed to the virus. If the danger was such that any infected health care worker was a risk to patients, then surely it would be in the interests of public safety to test all health care workers for HIV. The Department of Health do not stand by mandatory testing at this present time, which in essence means that if you are known to be HIV-positive then the basic right to work in the health care profession can be challenged and even withdrawn. This, I feel, is discrimination against only those known to be infected, and not those who practise ignorant of their status. It should be remembered that all practitioners and patients pose a potential infection risk and if that is the case then surely the same rules should apply to everyone regardless of their status being known.

THE RIGHT TO PRIVACY

Patient confidentiality is held as paramount in the medical profession. I believe that it is vital to maintain trust, on which effective care can be based. On the question of the right to privacy the Department of Health (1994) states in its document on the management of HIV-infected health care worker's that

> Patient safety and public confidence are paramount and dependent on the voluntary self declaration of the health care worker. Employers must promote a climate which encourages such confidential disclosure. It is thus extremely important that HIV-infected health care workers receive the same rights of confidentiality as any patient seeking or receiving medical care

Once again we find the guidance talking in terms of ideals. One only has to look at the popular press to see that whenever a health care worker has been infected by a patient their privacy is generally respected. They may only be described as 'a married female nurse' or 'a tragic midwife'. But when it comes to an infected health care worker being found to be positive, and particularly when a look-back exercise is being carried out, the popular press often reveal their name, lifestyle and whereabouts, microscopically displayed, often with photographs. If a health care worker behaved in this way towards a patient you can safely say that they would be suspended, disciplined and probably expelled from the medical or nursing profession.

The Press Complaints Commission states in its Code of Practice that if breaches of confidentiality can be justified in the wider public interest of safety then it is reasonable to report a story in such a way. I am inclined to agree with that statement; indeed we have a right to know about potential hazards, threats, or those who might want to harm us. Health care is a subject that affects everyone and it is obvious that if one is at risk in the health care setting we should know about it. This sort of information can then be used to avert those situations or help us to be especially aware of the hazards we may face.

There is a well known case in American psychiatry regarding the boundaries of confidentiality. The Tarasoff case was first heard in 1974, which held that psychotherapists had a duty to warn potential victims of violence. In 1976 the case was reheard, and the new ruling emphasized the therapist's responsibility to include a duty to protect and not merely to warn the victim (Joseph, 1991). The Tarasoff case concerned a psychiatrist who was found liable for not warning one young woman that one of his patients had threatened to kill her. After the patient – a young man – carried out his threat, the woman's family sued his doctor. The physician argued that the communication had been privileged, but the court disagreed. It considered the therapist's responsibility to protect the woman stronger than his duty to his patient to keep silent (Clark, 1991).

This case presents some very interesting points in relation to the HIV-infected health care worker. It could be argued that an HIV-infected health care worker posed such a threat that physicians who knew of their patient's HIV status and occupation as being one in the health care profession should have a moral obligation to inform hospital management and therefore break the confidentiality of the patient. Normally this wouldn't happen, but the physician could decide that such action was in the wider public interest. 'Many Doctors share the view that the public good comes first and no social problem illustrates the issue as sharply as HIV infection' (Clark 1991). HIV-infected health care workers have been portrayed as a hazard, and many of them have been publicly named and thrown out into the public domain. This is not justifiable in the public interest, as we know that the risk of HIV transmission from a health care worker to a patient is extremely unlikely. Yet the popular press have peddled fear and incited even more hatred. By breaching the confidentiality of health care workers they are providing their readers with a personality to hate. Is this an abuse of one's civil rights?

Article 17 of the International Covenant on Civil and Political Rights states that: 'No one shall be subjected to arbitrary or unlawful interference with his privacy, family, home or correspondence, nor to unlawful attacks on his honour and reputation' (Sieghart, 1989). An HIV-infected health care worker's antibody status should not be disclosed without the consent of the worker concerned. Any such action in my opinion is an unlawful interference with the worker's privacy. The case for the duty to warn and protect, i.e., disclosure in the wider public interest, is not justifiable because the risk of HIV transmission, even during exposure-prone procedures is minuscule. The right to privacy outweighs the risk involved and it is clearly not in the public interest to frighten them unnecessarily.

Indeed, 'Confidentiality protections encourage individuals to come forward for voluntary testing, counselling and research' and 'Discrimination against people affected by HIV is a major obstacle to public health efforts to halt the epidemic' (Cooper 1989).

Possible measures that would interfere with an individual's right to privacy are:

- mandatory testing for HIV;
- the compulsory registration of persons considered as likely to be infected with HIV, but who have not been individually tested;

- the mandatory collection, storage and processing by public authorities of personal information about those who are suspected or have been tested;
- making AIDS, or HIV-seropositivity, a 'notifiable disease';
- the disclosure of test results, or of other personal information held, to third parties;
- the criminalization of behaviour thought to be conducive to the spread of HIV.

(Sieghart, 1989)

Thankfully in the United Kingdom these measures are not policy. Although mandatory testing is not carried out in the health service, testing with consent is. The guidelines tell us that it is up to the individual if they believe themselves to be infected to seek diagnostic testing (Department of Health, 1994). This is stressed as being a matter of duty and personal responsibility. There is pressure on health care workers to do this. It is quite clear as it is a requirement of the guidelines. Consent for testing must be acquired by those taking and testing the blood sample. In giving consent one forfeits one's right to a degree of privacy and takes a chance that confidentiality will not be breached. The Department of Health reminds employers that they have the responsibility to ensure that 'HIV-infected health care workers receive the same rights of confidentiality as any patient seeking or receiving medical care' (Department of Health 1994). Lee Wugofski MD, MPH, director of the Center for Municipal Occupational Safety and Health, set up a confidential HIV counselling and testing programme for health care workers at San Francisco General Hospital. The system is designed to protect employees who are tested for HIV following occupational exposure to virus. Wugofski recommends that hospitals establish a locked, separate charting system for employees tested for HIV. At San Francisco General Hospital, HIV test results are kept separate from the other employee health charts. The charts are numerically coded and the only link to the health care worker's name is in a separate log book. Stickers with the health care worker's ID number are placed on lab tests, the tube of blood, and any form filled out by the employee. The employee's name should never be put on laboratory tests, Wugofski says. 'There is a good chance that someone in the clinical labs will know who the person is.' Access to results is limited to those providing counselling to employees and test results are only released to other parties after the health care worker has provided specific written consent (*AIDS Alert*, 1993).

There are some who claim that those with HIV, particularly health care professionals, should waive their right to privacy. Indeed, there are even those who would like to see the introduction of mandatory testing in the name of the wider public interest of safety. However, such infringements of the basic human right to privacy are not conducive to the public efforts to halt the epidemic. It is therefore in the wider public interest to make a real attempt to preserve that right.

THE RIGHT TO PROTECTION FROM DISCRIMINATION

AIDS discrimination almost always occurs because people are frightened or do not understand the fundamentals of HIV transmission. Discrimination is a way of distancing ourselves from something we do not want to associate ourselves with or become. Under US law HIV is considered to be a physical handicap, and therefore people infected with HIV or AIDS are protected against discrimination through laws written to protect the civil rights of handicapped and disabled citizens. The recent passage of the Americans with Disabilities Act strengthens federal protections against HIV-related discrimination. David Schuleman, supervising attorney of the AIDS and HIV discrimination unit in the Los Angeles City Attorney's Office, said those who are infected must 'be aware that there are federal, state and local laws that protect you from discrimination on the basis of your health status. Being infected with HIV does not give someone grounds to violate your rights' (*AIDS Alert*, 1990).

HIV has many faces; it can instil fear and prejudice and reinforce already negative ideas we have about certain groups of society. It can be and has been a weapon for political parties to use against whole sections of the community. The face of HIV can also be tolerance, as those wearing the red ribbons associated with AIDS awareness publicly display their tolerance. To some, HIV is a career; the 'HIV Industry' is a small pond full of big fish. It is a subject provoking extreme emotions whether you have the virus or not, whether you work in association with it or not.

In my experience as an HIV positive man, I have met people who have snatched my cup out of my hand and drunk from it to prove – I'm not sure what. People who hardly know me have hugged and kissed me. Others have avoided me or refused to shake my hand and said unkind things about me behind my back. But I must say that on the whole I have met with a positive response from most people. To a great extent that is because of the type of people I encounter and living in a city like London certainly helps.

AIDS has been an enriching experience in my life and has opened many doors for me. It has made me more introspective and I have developed personally because of it. That is my experience of having AIDS.

But what of other people's experience? Attitudes can be gauged through looking at different personal experiences of having HIV. Before we look at the attitudes an HIV-infected health care worker faces it is important that we look at general attitudes towards people living with HIV and AIDS.

The attitudes and prejudices within the health care profession towards HIV and those infected with it is much like the attitude we find outside. Fear of infection and the consequences it may bring might make us cautious with those with the virus. The fact that HIV primarily affects groups that some sections of society find difficult to tolerate can reinforce our negative ideas of them. 'Although the arrival of AIDS had not created an atmosphere of hostility and prejudice towards gay men and lesbians (that was already there), it had certainly provided bigots and moralists with material to back their beliefs' (Royal College of Nursing 1994). The Royal College of Nursing points out in its statement on the nursing care of lesbians and gay men that they recognize 'through work undertaken by its members that discrimination and prejudice towards lesbian and gay men exists in nursing'. It goes on to say that 'It is clear that lesbians and gay men have specific health care needs and concerns which nurses probably do not address'. If as the Royal College of Nursing states, discrimination exists against gay men within the health care profession, then people with HIV are clearly disadvantaged because the majority of people with HIV in the western world are gay.

Dr Adrian Rogers of the Conservative Family Campaign describes gay men and lesbians as being 'sterile, disease ridden and Godforsaken' (*Pink Paper*, 1995). My father's attitude was not too dissimilar. I know that growing up aware of his feelings about gay men caused me many problems in coming to terms with my sexuality. It is the same for many other gay men and lesbians. Some carry about their secret for years and sometimes for their entire lives. Fear of discrimination and what others think of them stops them from 'coming out'. In 1994 the legal age of consent was debated, resulting in a change in the law. The age of consent was dropped from 21 to 18. This was only a semi-victory. The fact remains that the age of consent is not equal with that of heterosexuals, effectively creating a divide between homosexuals and heterosexuals, although the divide has become smaller. Homosexuals are not entitled to the same rights that heterosexuals enjoy. Does this mean we are an 'under-class' and not worthy in the eyes of the powers that be? Occasionally speculation about the sexuality of certain members of the government arises. Would it be such a bad thing if some of them were gay? Would it affect their ability to work? I think not, yet many believe that 'coming out' would probably result in the destruction of their career.

We have all heard other people talking of 'undesirables', e.g. murderers, drug pushers, child molesters and queers. It is interesting how homosexuals are added to this infamous list. Homosexuality is seen by some people as being criminal and undesirable. AIDS has been described as the wrath of God on gays.

In an interview, Jerry Hayes MP for Harlow told me that there was a sea of change on the way, which he welcomed. He said that young people were far more tolerant and that homosexuality was just a fact of life not to be judged or be prejudiced against. I hope he is right. Positive gay and lesbian images are vitally important and the gay community have done much to project positive images. Famous people such as Elton John and Ian McKellen have done much to add to this image, though they are often ridiculed by the press. The courage of the gay community, particularly in these days of AIDS, is doing much to educate the younger generation and by so doing helping to dismantle the myths of homosexuality. This no one can ignore. However, the fact remains that homosexuals are blamed for the advent and spread of HIV, and some people believe that both are problems which need to be eradicated.

Discrimination results in the erosion of human rights. There are, however, certain influential groups who hold quite radical views on the rights of HIV-infected persons. Some clearly believe that HIV-infected people are not entitled to some of the basic human rights. One of these groups is the Conservative Family Campaign. In 1991 they created the 'HIV-Infected Citizen's Charter of Responsibility' in response to the Declaration of the Rights of People with HIV and AIDS. It is such an amazing document that it is reproduced here:

The Charter

All HIV-infected citizens have the following duties and responsibilities:

1. To recognize that they carry with them the potential to transmit HIV to others, and that they need to sacrifice personal freedoms (like others suffering from life threatening communicable diseases).
2. To abstain from acts of sodomy.
3. To abstain from all other risk-related sexual activity and to abstain from procreation for the sake of the unborn child.
4. To notify all sexual partners, current and previous where known.

5. To refrain from intravenous drug abuse.
6. To let their condition be notified to the appropriate medical authority, and to consent to comply with the recommendations of that medical authority even where this may involve restrictions on movement work or education.
7. To seek treatment for AIDS/HIV infection, and to accept that confidentiality may be breached when there is a risk of transmitting HIV or AIDS related pathogens e.g. tuberculosis, cryptococcal meningitis.
8. Not to work with food being consumed by members of the public especially the young, the frail, the infirm and the elderly, so as to avoid risk of transmitting AIDS related pathogens.
9. Not to donate blood, sperm or body organs.
10. To make their HIV status known if members of the nursing, medical or dental professions, and to give patients the choice whether to use their services.
11. To disclose their HIV status to employers or insurance companies, either to protect others from risk of infection, or to enable others to make informed decisions about employing or insuring them.
12. To accept prison authorities' precautions to protect uninfected prisoners from risk of infection.

(Conservative Family Campaign 1991)

In a press release the Conservative Family Campaign which is sponsored by, amongst others, 30 back bench Conservative MPs said:

> Liberal humanists and friends of the homosexual lobby have taken over policy in the Department of Health, emphasizing the rights of those infected with AIDS and HIV to the exclusion of their responsibilities, the precise opposite to conservative principles.
>
> At the same time, those whose debauched lifestyles led to them contracting HIV should take up the mantle of moral integrity. We urge them to contemplate their duties and responsibilities to the rest of society in line with the points raised in the Conservative Family Campaign Charter.

It is clear that those with debauched lifestyles in the eyes of the Conservative Family Campaign are homosexuals and IV drug users. This type of discrimination is found not only in the world of politics, but also in the health care setting, where professionals are sometimes as misinformed as everyone else. A survey in the United States concluded that discrimination in the medical profession results in substandard care for homosexual patients and career difficulties for gay and lesbian health care workers. The extent of the discrimination indicated that 56 per cent of practising physicians and 67 per cent of students reported such discrimination. More frightening still is the fact that 88 per cent reported hearing colleagues make disparaging remarks about homosexual patients (McCormick, 1994).

The *Pink Paper* reported that Dr Adrian Rogers, now chair of the Conservative Family Campaign, is standing for the Conservative Party at the next election. They quote Will Parry, a young man who has admitted that he had underage gay sex as saying: 'This is a man whose opinions are informed by prejudice and if he is elected then lesbians and gay men and many other groups are going to be completely disenfranchised from Parliament and it is a very dangerous prospect' (*Pink Paper* 1995) (Dr Rogers had demanded that he be arrested during a radio debate on the subject of the age of consent for homosexuals).

Jerry Hayes MP for Harlow resigned from the Conservative Family Campaign after they had published their Charter. Mr Hayes said that 'At a time when we should be educating young people of all sexual persuasions in their sexual behaviour, the suggestion that you should effectively criminalise the gay community is outrageous as it is counter productive' (Katz 1991). He also said 'I am quitting this organization and I would advise other MPs who are sponsors to do likewise. This report is offensive' (Fletcher 1991).

I interviewed Jerry Hayes in January 1995 at the House of Commons and he told me that he 'wouldn't mind being cared for by a nurse who he knew to be HIV-positive as long as they followed universal precautions'.

I thought it only right that I should give some members of the Conservative Family Campaign a chance to say what ever they wanted to on the subject of HIV health care workers. They declined to reply.

Attitudes of discrimination discourage people from being voluntarily tested for HIV. A study carried out by the University of California in San Francisco has found that individuals who lived in states with anti-discrimination laws were more likely to seek HIV testing (*AIDS Weekly* 1992). Surely an anti-discrimination approach and a protective environment would encourage more people to be tested voluntarily. It should be remembered that in the case of HIV-infected health care workers, the Department of Health rely on people to come forward voluntarily for the test. Certainly it is in the wider public interest that we nurture a safe and anti-discriminatory environment for all who are and potentially could be infected. If discrimination is a result of fear of the different or unknown, then perhaps we should look towards dispelling that fear and challenging those attitudes; and the health care setting would be a good place to start. The Code of Professional Conduct states that each registered nurse, midwife and health visitor should 'maintain and improve ones professional knowledge and competence' (UKCC 1991).

And rightly so, for only through education can we dispel the myths surrounding HIV and dismantle the prejudices and fears of those who have them.

References

AIDS Alert (1990) HIV-infected people protected against discrimination (includes related article on protecting your rights regarding insurance) (Common sense about AIDS). **5** (12), 229.

AIDS Alert (1993) How to ensure confidentiality of employee HIV tests (HIV post-exposure management: a guide for health care professionals). **8** (1), 16.

AIDS Weekly (1992) Study finds anti-discrimination laws increase voluntary HIV testing rates (8th International Conference on AIDS). p. 15. August.

Clark, Laura (1991) When – and when not – to protect patient privacy; AIDS, UR inquiries, and new reporting laws have complicated confidentiality. Here's how to steer clear of trouble. (Utilization review) (Includes story of instructing staff). *Medical Economics*, **68** (9), 95–9.

Conservative Family Campaign (1991) *HIV Infected Citizens' Charter of Responsibility*.

Cooper, Mike (1989) Study sees need for confidentiality, discrimination protection (American Bar Association's AIDS Coordinating Committee). *CDC AIDS Weekly*, August, p. 4.

Cosman, Teri and Bissell, Michael (1991) What has happened to patient confidentiality (Ethics in the clinical laboratory, Part 2). *Medical Laboratory Observer*, **23** (8), 38–41.

Department of Health (1994) *AIDS/HIV Infected Health Care Workers: Guidance on the Management of Infected Health Care Workers*. London: DoH.

Fletcher, D. (1991) Right-wing outrage over AIDS charter. *Daily Telegraph*, 27 August.

Joseph, David I. (1991) Confidentiality versus the duty to protect: foreseeable harm in the practice of psychiatry. *Journal of American Medicine*, **266** (3), 425.

Katz, I. (1991) Torn MP quits family group over HIV charter. *Guardian*, 27 August.

McCormick, Brian (1994) Anti-gay discrimination impedes careers, health care. *American Medical News*, **37** (26), 7.

Pink Paper (1995) Arrest Gays, Tory Doctor Stands for Parliament. 20 January.

Royal College of Nursing (1994) *Issues in Nursing and Health 26, The Nursing Care of Lesbians and Gay Men: An RCN Statement*. March.

Sieghart, P. (1989) *AIDS and Human Rights: A UK Perspective*. London: British Medical Association Foundation for AIDS.

UKCC (1991) *Code of Professional Conduct*. (2nd edn) London: UK Central Council of Nursing and Midwifery.

UKCC (1994) Acquired Immune Deficiency Syndrome and Human Immuno Deficiency Virus Infection (AIDS and HIV Infection), Annexe 1 to Registrar's letter 4/1994.

World Health Organization (1994) *Guidelines on HIV/AIDS in the Workplace. Series No. 7*. Geneva: WHO.

CHAPTER 5

Positive solutions: a nationwide project

Sarah Grice, Paul Mayho and Sue Morris

HIV/AIDS is a subject which now affects every country throughout the world. There are already millions of people known to be infected with the human immuno-deficiency virus (HIV). There are likely to be many more unknowingly infected with the virus, known to cause acquired immune deficiency syndrome (AIDS). Nurses as individuals have an invaluable role to play in many areas of health care provision for people affected by HIV/AIDS.
RCN Nursing Update, *HIV and AIDS: A Positive Response*

If nurses are to update and maintain their professional knowledge, how do we propose to do that? This chapter outlines a possible solution to counter discrimination and educate those in the front line, i.e. the nurses; it can be adapted to encompass other professionals involved in health care.

The project was devised with the help of Sue Morris SRN Dip N who formulated the local policy shown here which is now implemented at Crawley General Hospital where Sue works in GUM services. The education model that follows was devised by Sarah Grice who at the time of writing was a psychology student. Grice's model breaks new ground in peer advocacy and presents a fresh approach to educating health care professionals. I am very grateful to her for giving permission for her model to be used in this book.

This chapter was prompted by the total lack of any policy document within the NHS regarding nurses who are found to be HIV-positive. With an increase in negative media coverage about supposed transmissions to patients (there is only one case as discussed in Chapter 3, an American dentist who passed on the virus to patients and though proven through DNA strand testing according to the CDC in Atlanta, it is not known how the transmission occurred), and the fear within the health care profession regarding the professional responsibilities of antibody positive individuals, their colleagues and managers, there has been a clear call for guidelines to be developed. This chapter is an attempt to provide some solutions.

SUGGESTED LOCAL POLICY ON THE MANAGEMENT OF HIV-INFECTED HEALTH CARE WORKERS

Sue Morris, SRN Dip N

The Trust acknowledges the requirements to safeguard all employees and patients under its care from contracting blood-borne viruses, including HIV, and will ensure effective protective measures are put into practice. All workers are protected by the following acts and regulations:

- Health and Safety at Work Act 1974
- Control of Substances Hazardous to Health Regulations 1988
- Recommendations of the Department of Health Expert Advisory Group on HIV-Infected Health Care Workers March 1994
- Health Service Guidelines HSG (94)16

Purpose

- To ensure all health care workers are aware of policies and procedures relating to health care workers working with an HIV antibody positive status.
- To protect patients from the risk of acquiring HIV from an HIV-infected health care worker.
- To safeguard the interests of HIV-positive members of staff by providing them with advice, monitoring their health and ensuring relocation or retraining if necessary.

Practices

To implement the policy, the Trust will:
- Arrange for risk assessments to be undertaken to identify all exposure prone procedures (EPP)
- Provide information, instruction and training on how to safeguard the interests of the health care worker, the patient and the Trust.
- Make available the necessary resources to implement the policy.
- Annually review the policy and monitor its effectiveness.

Background Information

The Human Immuno-deficiency Virus (HIV) can be transmitted to patients or from patients via infected blood or body fluids.

There is a risk to staff through needle stick injury or splash to mucosa or broken skin.

There is a risk to patients through injury to a health care worker when 'the workers gloved hands may be in contact with sharp instruments, needle tips or sharp tissues (spicules of bone or teeth) inside a patient's open body cavity, wound or confined anatomical space where the hands or fingertips may not be completely visible at all times' (Department of Health, 1994).

Infection control

All employees are required to follow infection control procedures and adopt working practices to prevent HIV transmission in the health care setting, as advised in the *Infection Control Manual*. Health care workers who are antibody positive MUST NOT perform exposure-prone procedures.

EXPOSURE-PRONE PROCEDURES

EPPs are those where there is a risk that injury to the worker may result in the exposure of a patient's open tissues to the blood of the worker. These are defined as:

- Surgical entry into tissues, cavities or organs
- Repair of traumatic injuries
- Cardiac catheterisation and angiography
- Caesarian deliveries or obstetric procedures during which sharp instruments are used, e.g. episiotomy

Procedures for Implementation

1. All staff should follow general infection control guidelines and adopt safer working practices to prevent HIV transmission in the health care setting.
2. All staff with direct patient contact or who undertake exposure prone procedures have a responsibility to maintain the safety of their patients throughout these procedures, following Trust Policies and Statutory Acts of Law.
3. All accidents involving EPPs must be declared and documented. Staff must immediately present themselves to the Accident and Emergency Department for examination.
4. All staff who believe they may have been exposed to HIV must seek appropriate HIV antibody testing.
5. All staff should be made aware of the process by which to contact the Director of Public Health who should be notified of all HIV-infected health care workers who have performed exposure prone procedures.
6. The Occupational Health Department must promote a climate which encourages confidentiality and equal rights for HIV-infected health care workers.
7. An occupational health physician should be appointed who will advise on and monitor the health of the health care worker.
8. If the employee is unable to return to her or his normal area of work, alternative employment within the Trust should be provided with retraining where appropriate and feasible. Medical retirement should be considered as the last resort on the grounds of incapacity.
9. 'Look back' exercises should be considered only when the Director of Public Health feels it is appropriate and only after consultation with the Department of Health Expert Advisory Board. The interests of the health care worker should be considered and immediate practical and psychological support should be undertaken, including measures to protect privacy.
10. Every effort should be made to avoid disclosure of the health care worker's identity. Death of a health care worker should not end this duty of confidentiality.

HIV-INFECTED HEALTH CARE WORKERS

1. Staff diagnosed as HIV-antibody positive must immediately cease undertaking exposure prone procedures.
2. HIV-infected health care workers should immediately seek the advice of their Occupational Health Department concerning the monitoring of their health status, continuing work practices or reallocation within the Trust.
3. Independent legal advice sought by the health care worker should be respected, and the authority's legal advisors should maintain regular contact with those representing the health care worker.
4. HIV-infected health care workers should seek and receive support (practical or psychological) as appropriate to their needs.

AREAS OF RESPONSIBILITY

It is the responsibility of the management team of each directorate to:

1. Ensure that all staff in their area are aware of and comply with the requirements of the policy.
2. Provide the Occupational Health Department with an up-to-date list of all current staff undertaking exposure-prone procedures.

It is the responsibility of the Occupational Health Department to:

1. Provide a list for management teams of directorates identifying exposure-prone procedures.
2. Provide advice and support to a health care worker disclosing an HIV antibody positive diagnosis.
3. Ensure that the confidentiality of the infected health care worker is maintained.
4. Refer the health care worker to an appropriate specialist responsible for the management of monitoring their health.
5. Refer the health care worker to the Director of Public Health to assess whether reallocation is necessary.
6. Refer the health care worker to the Director of Public Health if they have undertaken exposure-prone procedures.

It is the responsibility of the Personnel Department to:

1. Support managers with specialist advice on employment law and procedures.
2. Facilitate training and induction programmes in conjunction with departmental managers, occupational health and clinical specialist to increase staff awareness of all health and safety policies.
3. Bring the policy to the attention of new health care workers, on behalf of their managers, in their contracts of employment.

EDUCATION
Sarah Grice BSc (Psychology)

The first part of this book outlines the rights and responsibilities of HIV-positive health care workers, the actual risk they pose in transmitting HIV to their patients, and the procedures that they can and cannot perform with absolute safety in the course of their working life after a positive diagnosis. It has also outlined what is, and what is not, appropriate behaviour for staff members working with an identified HIV-positive colleague, while stressing that 'it is likely that the majority of people infected with HIV are unaware of their infection' (Wenger *et al.*, 1994), and that 'it is every registered nurse's, midwife's and health visitor's responsibility to maintain and improve professional knowledge and competence' (UKCC, 1991).

Statistics collated by the PHLS Communicable Disease Surveillance Centre documenting reports of occupationally acquired HIV infection in health care workers in the UK up to May 1995, show that there have been four definite incidences of seroconversion after specific occupational exposure, and seven cases possibly occupationally acquired. Figures for the USA are 43 and 91 respectively. Many times this number however are HIV-infected, and even in 1993 it was estimated that there were 5800 health care workers with AIDS in the USA alone (Wicher, 1993). Despite these numbers of HIV-infected health care workers however, epidemiological studies (carried out for over ten years) have indicated that no transmissions to patients have occurred (Wicher, 1993). This is despite the fact that many of those who are HIV-positive (both those aware and those unaware of their HIV status) have carried out highly invasive procedures. In 1995 there is still not one case in Britain of HIV being transmitted by a health care worker to a patient.

There has been a focus on the responsibility of hospital and health authority personnel, yet there is a need for nurses to be made aware of the Department of Health guidelines and their own responsibility for observing them (Hart 1993a, b). As Wicher (1993) points out, there is still widespread discrimination against health care workers infected with HIV, and this is in part due to confusion about what the guidelines and recommendations are.

In an ideal world, implementations of the suggestions that have been made at the level of the individual staff member would require no more than a simple lecture or document relaying the facts. A more effective strategy is to identify and target factors that affect the comprehension and utilization of the information presented and to design an educational programme based on these factors, and not just on the information (the policy statement) that prescribes the specific change in behaviour that is desired. Maximum impact on behaviour and attitudes can then be achieved using the minimum of limited resources.

Every educational programme needs a communication system. For our purposes we shall examine four components.

1. Sender: the person, or group of people who originates the information.
2. Message: the information itself.
3. Channel: the mediator of the message.
4. Receiver: the person, or group of people, to whom the message is directed.

In order to most effectively balance the dynamics of the education programme in terms of the sender, the message and the channel, we need to look first at the characteristics of the receivers that could effect the efficacy of the programme.

As already discussed, the AIDS epidemic has been accompanied by intensely negative reactions to people presumed to be infected with HIV. This stigma is reflected in the constraints on the freedom of particular individuals and 'risk groups' even though this ultimately has no positive effect on the spread of the virus. A focus must be placed then on the social relationships in which a particular mark of shame or discreditation occurs; the way in which events are interpreted, affects and is affected by attitudes. These temporally stable mental positions often predict behaviour, unless situational pressures dictate otherwise. In practice this means that the attitudes of individual health care workers (who perceive themselves to be uninfected), towards individuals with HIV or AIDS, affects the type of behaviour change intervention that is effective.

People with AIDS are often wrongly perceived as putting others at risk. Even in the nursing profession there is a considerable lack of knowledge of the routes through which HIV transmission can occur, resulting in a fear of what is unknown.

There are three directions of transmission that induce fear:

1. Patient to nurse
Fear of contagion is common amongst health care workers (Currey *et al.*, 1990; Grossman and Silverstein, 1993). This may be due to a lack of knowledge about the real risk of transmission (Klimes *et al.*, 1990), but is not necessarily due to information being unavailable. It is often the fear produced by AIDS related stigma that inhibits the process of learning correct information. An educational programme needs to address the fears of health care workers and attempt to reduce anxiety levels before presenting information about the risk of transmission from patient to nurse and the behaviours that decrease this risk.

2. Nurse to patient
Nurses are legally bound to ensure the safety of their patients and to use universal precautions when engaging in exposure prone procedures. Workers known to be HIV-positive must not carry out these procedures. It is unfortunate that the latter precaution may reduce the risk perception of health care workers who are unaware of their own positive status and consequently increase the risk of HIV transmission to the patient through incautious practice. In these situations, fear of infection may not be high enough to prevent risk-taking behaviour.

Nurses who do know or suspect that they are HIV-positive may fear recrimination if they disclose their status to the authorities. This may discourage individuals from attempting to find out their own antibody status, and consequently result in antibody positive health care workers participating in exposure prone procedures.

An educational programme must address complacency and unprofessional behaviour by informing them of the routes of transmission, both occupationally and in daily life; stressing that most health care workers who are HIV-positive are unaware of their status; and reminding them of the legal and professional responsibilities, both of those who know their HIV status and those who believe themselves to be uninfected.

3. HIV-positive health care worker to uninfected colleague
In one postal survey 88 per cent of health care workers, out of a sample of 400 (including 300 nurses) were 'not worried' about working closely with a colleague diagnosed as being HIV-positive (Klimes *et al.*, 1990). The researchers do comment that this may represent an

'optimistic picture' due to methodological limitations of the study, 'self selection of respondents, and an effort to present oneself in a positive light'. Whatever the statistics are regarding the answers to a hypothetical question, the experience of many health care workers who are identified as HIV-positive, is of receiving negative responses both from their colleagues and the health authority.

An educational programme needs to present information about transmission risks from working with an HIV-positive health care worker to their colleagues: no risk unless unsafe sex or needle-sharing is engaged in at work!

I have outlined the fears about transmission, but why does the risk of HIV transmission induce such extreme reactions? Slovic (1987) outlines the characteristics of AIDS as an illness that evokes anxiety: it is new, fatal and caused by an unseen infectious agent that can remain intact in the body for an unknown period of time; it is perceived as 'out of control' and potentially catastrophic.

It follows then that a colleague with HIV/AIDS may confront others with their own mortality. Schutz (1962) suggests this provokes a 'fundamental anxiety', and argues that the 'natural attitude' is to construct experiences to avoid it. Stigmatization is an effective method of achieving this avoidance; it distances the 'uninfected' from death by defining the illness as an affliction of others.

An educational programme needs to provide insight into the real causes of behaviour which may not be obvious to the individual health care worker. It also needs to provide the health care worker with alternative ways of expressing anxiety which will not have the effect of increasing the risk of HIV infection, or of condemning individuals.

Stigma due to association with already stigmatized groups

It is true that, at least initially, AIDS has largely affected already stigmatized groups such as gay men and intravenous drug users. As an inevitable result, attitudes and reactions to HIV are inextricably linked with perceptions of the groups in which it is seen as being most prevalent, the stigma of disease and death becomes attached to the group itself. By a process of misguided generalization, people with AIDS have become further divided into the 'blameless victim' (those supposedly infected by the HIV-positive health care worker) and the 'blamable victim' (the HIV-positive worker, who furthermore, is often presumed to be gay).

One of the areas that needs to be addressed is the stigmatization of people with AIDS. The breakdown of barriers of fear and complacency must be attempted in order that personal and social risk assessment is more realistic. Knowledge about the facts of HIV and AIDS may then be assimilated, and the awareness of the health care worker about how they are affected by the normative attitudes of their social reference groups, may be raised.

The characteristics so far are summed up by Carlisle (1994) as 'ignorance and fear'. These are important issues to address, but there are other characteristics that need to be identified. Health care workers cannot in real terms be defined as a unitary body in their attitudes. Subgroups can be identified by the way health care workers deal with working with HIV-infected people, whether patient or colleague. They tend to respond in three basic ways (Eakin and Taylor 1990): avoidance, they distance themselves from it; engagement, they involve themselves in AIDS work; and adaptation, they accommodate to AIDS work.

The needs of these three groups differ in what they require from an AIDS education programme. Those distancing themselves from AIDS work physically and mentally are the group we have already discussed, who hold prejudicial attitudes or phobias and are likely to have the least accurate knowledge about HIV. Rippetoe and Rogers (1987) found this 'denial' to be the most maladaptive to a health threat. Individuals who use it may have an inaccurate conception of their own and others' infection risk and have 'weakened intentions to adopt the adaptive response'. They are also the hardest to get to attend any kind of workshop or lecture (Rudd, 1993).

The second group, the 'engagers' need to be targeted for the alleviation of mental health issues that include coping with death and dying, work overload, burnout and depression (Grossman and Silverstein 1993)

The third group, the 'adapters' are the group in which instigation of attitude and behaviour change is most straightforward. These health care workers tend to be less prejudiced towards people with AIDS than 'avoiders' and less likely to suffer from work overload and burn out than 'engagers'. This means that the barriers to learning are less rigid than in the other groups, but effective training and support must be provided.

The solution

The target group has been discussed in detail in order to tailor the message, the medium and the sender to the characteristics of the receiver.

The message that needs to be communicated is, at the most basic level, the content of the local policy document, yet as has been discussed the characteristics of health care workers as a group mean that there are various barriers of fear and of prejudice affecting the implementation of the policy at the individual level. Research has indicated the methods that are most effective at surmounting these barriers, while presenting the information in an understandable and cost-effective way.

Suggestions to promote implementation of policy at the level of the individual worker

It is essential that all health care professionals are aware of the contents of the policy and their own professional duty to observe the policy recommendations.

If attendance of workshops is voluntary, then how do we encourage those people described as 'avoiders' to attend them? This is a particularly difficult issue regarding community-based health care workers, or those working in a small practice with low HIV prevalence. Avoiders have been found to be the most difficult health care workers to reach (Rudd, 1993). They include those who believe that HIV and AIDS are something that they don't have to deal with. They may be 'phobic' of either people who are gay, or of the HIV illness itself, in which case the advertisement of a workshop or a study day may provoke high anxiety. They may have an accurate knowledge of HIV and transmission and are aware of the problem of social stigma but do not translate this awareness into individual cautionary behaviour, due to a falsely low perception of risk, or the belief that 'it won't happen to me'. They may believe that they have contracted HIV previously, either due to behaviour at work, or at home, but use avoidance strategies to attempt to cope with their fear and anxiety.

ADVERTISING

The programme needs to be promoted in a way that appeals to all health care workers. This can be by way of flyers and posters around the workplace, at professional meetings and at conferences appealing to legal responsibilities not just of the establishment but of the individual. The motivation to change attitudes by means of social influence is partly mediated by the perceived power of the source over the individual. This power can be based on the legal right of the source to prescribe a certain behaviour and/or the ability of the source to enforce punishment. Emphasizing the legal or professional duty of the health care worker to know and apply the contents of the policy document is the most likely to attract the individual worker.

Another method of promoting the programme is to create a liaison procedure with the staff of each individual health care setting, perhaps by using key informants of standard position within the setting, e.g. ward sister, staff nurse and so on. This has a two-fold purpose;

1. To conduct a needs assessment and target characteristic attitudes within each institution resulting in a programme better tailored to the target group (Rudd 1993).
2. To involve health care workers at each institution and in this way capitalize on the ability of the existing social network to promote positive attitudes.

It is essential that education is provided not only to those health care workers already qualified in their profession, but to those who are in training or in university. In this case it is easier to achieve compulsory attendance by incorporating it into the existing lecture programme. The actual programme however, will fundamentally be the same, and can still involve needs assessment procedures and liaison with students through elected informants.

The Message

A programme that aims to educate health care workers about the contents of a policy regarding behaviour in relation to AIDS issues must involve:

1. Opportunity for discussion and an outlet for expression of the fears of the health care worker. Information regarding a specific group designed to discuss and address these fears when the intervention or study day is over.
2. Repeated statements of the ways in which HIV is transmitted and how it is NOT transmitted.
3. Repeated statements of the risks that an HIV-positive health care worker poses to patients and colleagues.
4. Discussion of personal issues raised through working closely with an individual with a terminal illness.
5. Discussion of practical methods to reduce infection risk, e.g. how to most effectively start an IV while wearing gloves.
6. Discussion of AIDS related stigmas, where stigmas originate, the role of the society in reinforcing stigmas.
7. Raising of awareness of the effect that stigmas have on the stigmatized individual and those stigmatizing. (Likelihood of increase in personal risk of infection by unrealistic

risk perception and resulting behaviour.) Discussion of the relationship of personal risk assessment to actual risk behaviours.

8. Social support for changing of attitudes and behaviours.
9. Discussion of personal responsibilities to patients and colleagues who are perceived to be HIV-positive.
10. Destruction of common myths, e.g. that it is possible to see if someone is infected with HIV.

The source

The most effective source of information in an educational programme about AIDS is an HIV-positive person who discloses their positive status to the group. Scollay *et al.* (1992) states that this is an 'essential part of HIV/AIDS education program aimed at altering behaviour.' It is also advocated by many other researchers in the field (Rundell *et al.* 1993). It is clear that an HIV-positive person could fulfill many of the requirements of the persuasive educator outlined above. Scollay *et al.* (1992) suggest two more specific reasons: an HIV-positive person can implicitly challenge the misconception that HIV is identifiable by sight, and that an HIV-positive person automatically qualifies as a 'patient'. An HIV-positive person can explicitly interrupt 'avoidant thinking' by personalizing the HIV/AIDS problem in an externally unavoidable way. A health care worker who also happens to be HIV-positive can challenge this even more powerfully by appealing to the similarities between him/her and the group, especially by being experienced in the practical problems involved in implementing policy requirements. An added advantage is that as health care workers they are experienced in using the professional language of health care professionals, thus adding to the perceptions of familiarity and similarity.

The channel

The issue of stigma, and the awareness of the forms of AIDS-related stigmas in the health care profession that have been outlined here, should be used in an educational programme as a vehicle for discussing the roots of fear and negative behaviour towards people with HIV. This can form the basis for the discussion of the importance of social influence, both in initiating and sustaining AIDS-related stigma and in influencing personal risk perception, including the behaviours that are often associated with this. It is possible to point out the role of the workplace and work colleagues in providing social referencing and support, and the possibly devastating effects of withdrawing social support or using the power of the social network negatively.

The beginning and the end of any educational session should summarize the objectives and conclusions of the session, in order to capitalize on the primary and recency effects of memory. The important points of the policy document and personal responsibility for acting in accordance with its requirements, must be stressed. As Mcguire (1969) points out, conclusions must be drawn and alternative arguments negated to inoculate against negative attitude change.

Research has shown that the most effective method of achieving maximum retention of the information presented in a seminar is through active participation of those attending the session. This can be approached in two ways:

1. Giving participants time to interview the health educator about HIV. (Scollay *et al.*, 1992)
2. Giving participants opportunity for feedback in the form of a questionnaire about the content of the session, the way it was delivered and so on, and the opportunity to discuss the session with the key informant. Both act as memory aids.

The session should be divided into five parts:

1. Presentation of the information of the policy by the HIV-infected health care worker (health educator).
   Brief discussion of the role of stigma and the social construction of attitudes.
   Personal experience of being HIV-positive and the treatment by co-workers.
2. Interview by the health care workers with the health educator after the presentation and talk.
3. Discussion in small groups about the issues raised, particularly the affective issues of coping with fear, working with people who are HIV-positive, anger, loss, depression and death.
4. Reiteration of the facts of transmission of HIV and the personal responsibility of each health care worker.
5. Discussion of support groups, telephone lines, counselling and HIV testing.

The length of sessions varies and should be targeted for individual institutions. The programme could be covered in a one-day workshop. However, sessions of one or two hours may be most attractive to health care workers who attend out of the desire to find out their legal obligation. It may be possible to present several short sessions over a number of weeks if an initial attendance raises further issues that the health educator feels it necessary to address.

It is important to monitor the success of the health education programme and to establish a feedback loop that can suggest possible changes. Health education and the changing of attitudes and behaviours are two of the chief interests of social and health psychology. The implementation of policy suggestions at the level of the individual health care worker can call on research findings to devise a programme that is likely to achieve the most consistent and stable change in behaviour and attitude. The one outlined here is based on an amalgamation of traditional theory and social psychological research into the characteristics of health care workers and the results achieved by other AIDS/HIV educational programmes. It provides a basis on which to build a more comprehensive programme targeted at specific health care settings.

References

Carlisle, D. (1994) Psycho-social care of HIV positive people. *Nursing Standard*, **8** (18) 37–40.

Currey, C.J., Johnson, M. and Ogden, B. (1990) Willingness of the health-professions students to treat patients with AIDS. *Academic Medicine*, **65** (7) 472–4

Department of Health (1994) *AIDS/HIV Infected Health Care Workers: Guidance on the Management of Infected Health Care Workers*. London: HMSO.

Eakin, J.M. and Taylor, K.M. (1990) The psycho-social impact of AIDS on health care workers. *AIDS*, **4** Suppl (1), 5257–62.

Grossman, A.H. and Silverstein, C. (1993) Facilitating support groups for professionals working with people with AIDS. *Social Work*, **38** (2), 144–51.

Hart, S. (1993a) Infection control: HIV and the health care worker (Part 1). *Nursing Standard*, **7** (45), 38–9.

Hart, S. (1993b) Infection control: HIV and the health care worker (Part 2). *Nursing Standard*, **7** (46), 29–30.

Klimes, J., Catalan, J., Bund, A. and Day, A. (1990) Knowledge of attitudes of health care staff about HIV infection in a health district with low HIV prevalence. *AIDS Care*, **1** (3), 313–20.

McGuire, W.J., (1969) The nature of attitudes and attitude change. In A. Tajfel and D. Fraser (eds) (1991) *Introducing Social Psychology* London: Penguin.

Rippetoe, P.A. and Rogers, R.W. (1987) Effects of protection-motivation theory on adaptive and maladaptive coping with a health threat. *Journal of Personality and Social Psychology*, **52** (3), 596–604.

Rudd, R.E. (1993), Evaluator collaboration across diverse AIDS related educator programs. *Evaluation Practice*, **14** (3), 243–53.

Rundell, J.R., Ursano, R.J. and Sasaki, J. (1993) Effectiveness of an educational intervention session in challenging attitudes and beliefs about HIV: impact of an interview with an HIV-infected physician. *Academic Psychiatry*, **17** (4) 202–7.

Schutz, A. (1962) Multiple realities. In M. Nataanson (ed.), *Collected Papers: Vol. 1, The Probability of Social Reality*. The Hague: Nijhoff, 207–59.

Scollay, P., Doucett, M., Perry, M. and Winterbottom, B. (1992) AIDS education of college students: the effect of an HIV-positive lecturer. *AIDS Education and Prevention*, **4** (2), 160–71.

Slovic, P. (1987) Perception of risk. *Science*, 236, 280–5.

Wenger, N.S., Kusseling, F.S. and Shapiro, M.F. (1994). When patients first suspect and find out they are infected with HIV: implications for prevention. *AIDS Care*, **6** (4), 399–410.

Wicher, C.P. (1993) AIDS and HIV: the dilemma of the health care worker. *Todays OR Nurse*, **5** (2), 14–22.

UKCC (1991) *Code of Professional Conduct*. London: UK Central Council for Nursing, Midwifery and Health Visiting (2nd edn).

Part Two:

Attitudes and Their Consequences

Introduction: attitudes and their consequences

Part Two deals with the attitudes of others towards those with HIV and the consequences of them. Ever since the emergence of HIV there has been a generally negative reaction to people with the virus and a new surge in prejudice towards the social groups the virus seems primarily to affect. Naturally a potentially killer virus loose in the world is a frightening prospect. For many years now as medicine has advanced new treatments, vaccines and even cures for infections and viruses that only 100 years ago or less were killing people have become commonplace, although admittedly many illnesses remain uncured or even untreatable. In the western world, many infectious diseases have been virtually eradicated because of improved hygiene, sanitation and developments in research.

So, were we becoming complacent, thinking that we finally were beginning to conquer nature? On 5 June 1981, the *Morbidity and Mortality Weekly Report* (1981) carried an article reporting five cases of pneumocystis carinii pneumina (PCP) in homosexual men. Later, other cases were reported in other major US cities and so heralded the arrival of AIDS. Within a short space of time homosexuals started dying in the UK. The British press were quick to offer theories on the disease and they expressed very little compassion for those who were dying of it. The public, so used to science being able to treat, vaccinate and cure most of the old infectious diseases, started to worry about catching the virus themselves. Could it be caught by breathing the same air as someone with AIDS or from cutlery and crockery? At first no one really knew. Those with the virus were treated and cared for under very stringent infection control procedures. Eventually with the discovery of a retro-virus which was named HIV we became more aware of its transmission routes. The infection control procedures were relaxed for those ill with AIDS as the health care community better understood the virus' transmission routes. The public, however, were slower to respond to the public information campaigns assuring the masses that there were certain ways one could contract HIV and casual contact was not one of them. Even today, many people are still frightened of contracting HIV although most people have some sort of idea as to the possible modes of transmission.

The morality concerning the transmission of HIV has been an issue for many. Right-wing groups and individuals suggested that homosexuals and those with AIDS should be quarantined. One senior police officer suggested that it was God's punishment on those who led debauched lifestyles.

With the development of surveillance systems in the mid 1980s we began to get a better picture of what was actually going on. The HI virus was spreading not only amongst homosexuals, but also amongst other sections of our society. Infection amongst heterosexuals was seen to be increasing and the potentiality of a possible world-wide human catastrophe was realized. Figures and future estimates of numbers of infected people world-wide were bandied about. Those figures we have discovered are not as high today as was originally predicted. We have since learnt that there are ways of protecting ourselves and others from the virus. The government, realizing that the wider community were potentially open to infection with HIV, finally kicked into action with a public health campaign. Leaflets were posted to every household in the UK and the infamous iceberg and tombstone ads became a warning to everyone. Not everyone felt that the modes of transmission were effectively conveyed by the campaign. HIV prevention organizations and self-help groups started up. Part of their remit and aim was to challenge the discrimination that people with the virus faced and educate the public about the transmission risks.

In 1985 the world was shocked by the death of Rock Hudson from AIDS and we started to realize that HIV could infect anyone and had no respect for wealth or social position. Since then other famous and well-loved people have also died. The rich and famous and even royalty lost friends from the disease. They started to come out in force and support openly those with the virus. The press printed pictures of the Princess of Wales shaking the hands of people with AIDS and hugging them, which had a very positive effect on the attitude of the population towards those with the virus.

It is good that attitudes are changing, but prejudice has by no means disappeared. Terry Dicks MP declared in a Commons debate that HIV was a 'self-inflicted lovies disease that had decimated the arts world'.

The dilemma of the HIV-infected health care worker continuing in practice has been a problem in terms of assuring the health service users that they are not at risk. I believe this is possibly because other HIV information has concentrated on taking measures to protect oneself. Also the public understand that HIV is blood-borne, and often in the health care setting there is a probability of bleeding and spattering.

Another factor that may have caused difficulty in getting the right messages across to the population is that many of the prevention methods advocated give the individual much of the control over the possibility of contracting the virus, whereas in the case of contact with a health care worker we place ourselves in their care and entrust to them our safety. Often we may be unconscious and totally dependent on the health care worker to care for us. The problem may be that we find it difficult to trust those who care for us in times of bad health and emergency. As was stated in Part One, effective care can be based only on trust.

Many people believe that HIV is something that people bring on themselves, and the thought of being infected by one of those people fills them with horror. Our attitudes toward people with HIV and AIDS can have very negative consequences on those with the virus. On the other hand, the discrimination directed towards social groups primarily affected with the virus has had a unifying effect on them. Leaving AIDS politics and the internal bickering and personality disputes of those in the HIV sector to one side, we generally can stand side by side and state that we are working to dismantle the prejudice and attitudes towards the virus.

As the HIV pandemic becomes older, perhaps people will not see it as such a threat and accept it as any other disease that one may be stricken by. There is no doubt in my mind that having HIV or AIDS carries a lot more baggage than diseases such as, for example, cancer or leukaemia, which over the years we have come to accept as a 'potentiality' for anyone and now have some sympathy for those with the disease.

If we are to try to change attitudes then we must look at where they have come from, who fuels them and try to establish some empathy with the feelings and consequences of those attitudes.

Reference

Morbidity and Mortality Weekly Report (1981) Centres for Disease Control: pneumocystis pneumonia – Los Angeles. **30**, 250–2.

CHAPTER 6

Portrayal of HIV-positive health care workers by the British press

Clearly the health reporters we talked to see their AIDS reporting as a two edge sword, yet despite their ambivalence, our findings suggest that reporters believe they have been doing a thorough job in covering AIDS.

(Dr Kenneth Rabin)

The first part of this book has looked at the rights and responsibilities of HIV-infected health care workers. It was suggested throughout that misinformation resulted in prejudice and fear and that much of the misinformation has served only to reinforce already negative attitudes towards those groups of people who are primarily affected by HIV. This chapter will examine the media's role in dissemination of inaccurate information.

In the first instance I must acknowledge that the media are not the sole source of misinformation. Sometimes an idea or suggestion can be taken out of context, and as in a game of Chinese whispers, the idea is embellished, the original facts turning into myths. I do, however, believe that the press in Britain have been central to the peddling of misinformation, with no thought for the consequences.

The mass media are increasingly recognized by those concerned with educating the public as offering an extremely effective channel for communicating health messages. But there is evidence to suggest that the media, particularly the tabloid press, have failed in effectively communicating the health messages with regard to HIV as a whole and in particular to the continued practice of HIV-infected health care workers.

The supposed dilemma of HIV-infected health care workers continuing to practise came to the public's attention after Florida dentist David Acer was reported to have infected five of his patients. It made worldwide headlines and resulted in a panic over the possibility of being cared for by an HIV-infected health care worker. Calls were made and are still being made for the mandatory testing and dismissal of HIV-infected health care workers and the British press have had an ample supply of health care workers to fuel their crusade against those who are positive.

If a reminder was needed that among infectious diseases AIDS/HIV is a special case as far as the media are concerned, the furore over HIV-positive health care workers amply supplies it. AIDS/HIV continues to have the power to whip up irrational fear and blind prejudice in journalists in a way that nothing else does. Sensational media reporting has done incalculable damage to the general education and information programme on AIDS/HIV; those in all the caring professions who have been involved in AIDS/HIV education over the past 10 years could be forgiven for thinking they have been wasting their time. (*Nursing Times*, 1993)

It would make sense to conclude that the media are not a good way of educating the public when it comes to the subject of HIV and AIDS. If this disease is an exception to the rule then it has been a mistake for public information campaigns to have been conducted through the popular press. 'Most governments reporting cases of HIV and AIDS to the World Health Organization have now conducted public information campaigns on the subject mainly through the mass media' (Tavanyar 1992). Even so, if the media have not disseminated facts I believe they have very effectively manipulated public opinion.

HIV AND AIDS JARGON

To examine the British press' reporting on HIV-infected health care workers it will help to establish some principles of AIDS reporting.

It is easy to spot comments made by journalists that might make a difference as to how the reader perceives those infected with HIV and AIDS. One can always judge the standard of a journalist's work and their personal knowledge of HIV by their use of the jargon that comes packaged with HIV and AIDS. Admittedly we enter the realms of political correctness here, and it is easy to see how people can become agitated when the jargon is used incorrectly. (I am probably guilty of this myself on occasion.)

Some of the terms journalists use are offensive to people with HIV and AIDS and can cause discord amongst those with the virus and organizations who work to improve awareness. To deliver the message, so to speak, we can improve our use of certain phrases. Here follows a crash course in 'AIDS Jargon';

AIDS (confused with HIV): AIDS stands for Acquired Immuno Deficiency Syndrome and occurs when a person's immune system is seriously damaged by HIV. The term AIDS should not be used to describe anyone who has not had an opportunist infection as listed by the World Health Organization, such as PCP, CMV or Karposi Sarcoma. A better alternative is HIV infection or HIV-positive.

AIDS victim: A widely used phrase. Many people feel this implies powerlessness and that they have no control over their lives. Many prefer the phrases HIV-positive person, person with AIDS or PWA.

AIDS sufferer: For very much the same reasons as the phrase AIDS victim, the same alternatives apply.

AIDS carrier: This term is highly stigmatizing and can only contribute to the prejudice that exists already. You cannot 'catch AIDS'; the effective agent is the HI virus and AIDS is a definition of a stage in the illness that more often than not leads to death.

Innocent victims: This in some way implies that there are guilty parties in the AIDS equation. 'Innocent victims' in the eyes of the press may be people who have contracted the virus medically, e.g., haemophiliacs using Factor 8, or children and babies born with the virus where it is passed on by the mother. I suggest that this phrase is one of the most damaging. To apportion blame is futile and does not help society to look for solutions and acceptance of those who have the virus.

General population: This phrase suggests that the 'high risk' groups are not part of the general population. It creates a division between those who are infected and those who are not. It also wrongly implies that certain minority groups are to blame, rather than behaviour which is a crucial factor in HIV transmission.

High risk groups: Again, this implies that membership of a particular group, rather than behaviour, is the significant factor in HIV transmission. A good alternative is 'affected communities', which presents a more positive sympathetic approach.

Bodily fluids: The most important thing here is to be specific. Tears, sweat, saliva and urine do not carry enough HIV in concentration to a be transmission risk.

AIDS patient: This should only be used to describe someone who has AIDS and who is, in the context of the story, in a medical setting such as a hospital or hospice. The alternatives are the same as for AIDS victim/sufferer/carrier.

By taking more care and using the correct terminology we stand more of a chance in successfully creating a more sensitive awareness.

ANALYSIS OF TABLOID PRESS REPORTING ON HIV AND HEALTH CARE WORKERS

HIV has been reported as more than a medical condition; the disease as a punishment for 'immoral' behaviour has become clearly defined. Those who believed HIV was a disease of the underclass were shocked in 1985 when photographs appeared of the late Rock Hudson and his death because of AIDS was reported. It proved that HIV has no respect for wealth and privilege. Unlike many misguided souls the HIV virus does not prejudge, it does not selectively target, anyone will do. Morality in transmission of the virus and the way it is reported varies from case to case. Those infected through blood products and babies born with the virus became the 'innocent victims', implying that homosexuals or IV drug users were the guilty parties. Instead of examining the clinical issues surrounding the virus, we are bogged down in the morality of transmission. As discussed in chapter four, the Conservative Family Campaign implies in its Charter on the responsibilities of people with HIV, that those infected are so as a result of a debauched lifestyle. This suggests that HIV is a punishment in the moral sense.

It is a waste of time apportioning blame as to where the virus came from. That is no comfort for those who have the virus, nor does it help to alleviate the obstacles faced by one who has the virus. 'We should take a lead from President Kaunda, whose own son died of AIDS, when he says that we must focus not on where AIDS came from, but on where it is going.'

For the past ten years, newspapers have apportioned blame. Insensitive, biased reporting and misinformation has helped to mould the prejudices of the public, probably more so than any other medium. An example of this is the coverage of the case of an HIV positive homosexual doctor and who was allowed to continue practising. The *Daily Star* (2 September 1993) reports:

Any doctor with AIDS should have the decency and sense to stop practising. No one would let a GP or consultant come within ten yards, knowing there was a risk of catching this horrific disease.

But the medical profession looks after its own.

Colleagues of a gay specialist who caught AIDS from his boyfriend are backing his fight to keep on working. They are even hiding the identity of this walking time bomb, whose patients are being kept totally in the dark. If a doctor had typhoid or virulent TB, there would be no question of his treating people.

But AIDS is different. The gay lobby has succeeded in making it a politically correct illness.

It's a shameful conspiracy which should be blown wide open.

This article reeks of the ghost of 'gay plague' journalism which haunted us back in the early and mid 1980s. It has all the qualities of exactly the type of opinion on the subject of HIV/AIDS that we have come to expect from the tabloid press.

In the words of the *Daily Star* 'It's a shameful conspiracy which should be blown wide open.' Let's do just that and go back through the article pointing out the technical mistakes and the judgemental words.

In the first sentence we are told that any doctor with AIDS should be sensible enough to stop practising. According to the *Daily Star* this man does not have the decency to do this. This statement implies that it is not sensible and is dangerous to continue practising, and that in doing so this particular doctor is risking the lives of his patients. The doctor, incidentally, was only infected with the HIV virus and did not have AIDS. He was healthy enough to continue working.

The next sentence clearly states that anyone wouldn't go 'within ten yards, knowing that there was a risk of catching this horrific disease'. I find this very frightening. After years of trying to educate the population about the transmission routes of HIV and how they can avoid infection, we find ourselves in a situation where it is suggested that even coming 'within ten yards' of an infected person is dangerous. I will never travel on the tube again.

Of course the medical profession are to blame, according to the next statement. 'The medical profession looks after its own.' This hardly portrays trustworthiness on the part of the medical profession. The reader is encouraged to believe that the profession is more interested in looking after its members than its patients. Trust, a vital component in delivering effective care, is diminished.

We are told that the doctor concerned 'caught AIDS' from his boyfriend. Technically you do not catch AIDS, you acquire HIV. The assumption is made that the doctor's boyfriend passed the virus onto him in the first place, effectively blaming the boyfriend for passing it on. GUILTY!

The doctors colleagues are 'hiding the identity' of the doctor concerned. This is more than likely based on the fact that the journalist concerned, despite trying various methods of finding out the name of the doctor, failed.

The same paragraph calls the doctor a 'walking time-bomb'. This is most certainly incorrect. This doctor will not infect even one patient, so long as he follows the guidance that applies to his profession and the nature of the procedures he carries out. We are told that his patients are 'completely in the dark' to this horror that is threatening them. The implication of secrecy surrounding the story is very distressing, it does not inspire confidence. This doctor may as well be the Grim Reaper.

The journalist is obviously unaware of the transmission routes of the HIV virus. He states that 'If a doctor had typhoid or virulent TB, there would be no question of his treating people.' I should hope not. These diseases can be transmitted just by breathing on someone. The same cannot be said of HIV.

Anyhow at least there were no spelling mistakes.

In the story of a nurse who contracted the HIV virus through a needle stick injury we find a different approach. The report is more sensitive because of the route of transmission of the virus. In this example the woman concerned was married and therefore, in some people's view, an 'innocent victim'. Both the doctor and the nurse had the same virus, yet the means of transmission in the doctors case, i.e. suggested as his lifestyle, is in the newspaper's opinion morally wrong.

The story about the HIV-positive nurse did not receive as much coverage as the report about the doctor. In most of the tabloids the article was small and could easily have been missed. The *Today* newspaper reported the incident like this:

A nurse has caught the AIDS virus after treating an infected patient.

The married woman cut herself while helping to resuscitate a woman diagnosed HIV-positive eighteen months earlier.

The 59-year old nurse is the second health care worker in Britain to be infected by a patient.

Medics may now call for routine testing of patients. (*Today*, 1993).

There is little that is wrong technically with this article, although the fact that the woman contracted the virus in the line of duty and is married suggests that the nurse concerned did not deserve to contract the virus and is an innocent victim. It is a terrible thing that this woman contracted HIV; I hope that life treats her better in the years to come. I feel the same way about the homosexual doctor; he did not deserve to contract HIV either and the same wishes go out to him. No one deserves HIV. The factor we see illustrated by these stories is that the lifestyle of those infected, the way we live our lives and how we contracted the virus in the first place, is the topic of debate, not the disease itself. These articles clearly portray innocent and guilty parties. This can only contribute to prejudice, discrimination, blame and hatred.

In January 1995 the *Tonight* newspaper, a free newspaper distributed to London commuters, declared in a headline that took up three times as much room as the article itself that there was a 'Hunt for 1300 AIDS Dentist's Patients'. The first sentence implied that two London Health Authorities were desperately trying to trace more than 1,300 patients following the death of a dentist, who died of an AIDS related illness. The article's last sentence quoted John James, chief executive of Kensington and Chelsea and Westminster Health Commissioning Agency as saying that the chances of patients having contracted the virus were 'minuscule'. And rightly so. However, such a story is not worthy of front page headlines considering the negligible risk of transmission. It seems that HIV-infected health care worker scare stories are still very newsworthy. I repeatedly tried to contact the Editor of the newspaper to ask her to justify this story being front-page news. She declined to reply.

The *People* newspaper featured a story about the same dentist five days after *Tonight*. It devoted its first five pages to the story. A front-page headline above a photograph of the dentist and another doctor posing in party outfits reads; 'Kiss of Death!' The text next to it reads: 'A dead dentist and a dying doctor. Inside the perverted world of two men who got AIDS and betrayed their patients.'

The *People* declared that 'the disturbing facts of this case will spark a national outcry'. What facts? The article merely creatively described the fast lives of the dentist and doctor concerned, who according to the *People* 'rubbed shoulders with royalty and moved effortlessly through high society . . . but behind the curtain of respectability lay a sleazy world involving a conveyor belt of gay sex partners'.

The *People* depicted the Department of Health and Virginia Bottomley as being evasive. In another subtitle they asked 'Why won't you give us an answer, Bottomley!' They then went on to print their questions and printed the answers from the Department of Health for their readers to 'judge'. The answers from the Department of Health obviously were not sufficient for the *People* newspaper who set up a telephone poll to find out if their readers thought that there should be mandatory testing for health care workers. The *People*, in calling for mandatory testing for all health care workers, said 'AIDS makes them unfit to practice which is why they must have compulsory tests and if infected kept away from patients.' (*People* 1995).

A spokesperson told the *Pink Paper* of the *People*'s coverage: 'It is perhaps what one would expect from that paper' (*Pink Paper*, 1995). The *People*'s story is a prime example of the dangerous media coverage that instills prejudice and fear, and may cost people their lives. The most frightening example of this is misinformation about transmission risks. As we do not have a vaccine against the HIV virus or any cure or effective treatment against the progression of it, our only real defence is stemming it at the routes of transmission. Therefore people need to be very clear as to what these are so that they can protect themselves. Despite the headline, 'Kiss of Death', one cannot contract HIV from kissing or any other casual contact. In the same way, to portray HIV-infected health care workers as being a 'high risk' to patients is equally damaging. The *People* listed '14 Deadly Cases' that had 'rocked' the health service. This is completely misleading. HIV-infected health care workers are not considered to be a risk as long as universal precautions are observed and known HIV-infected health care workers do not carry out exposure-prone procedures, as mentioned in previous chapters. HIV-infected health care workers pose only a hypothetical potential risk to patients, not a 'Deadly' one.

I asked the editor of the *People*, Bridget Roe, to justify why this story took up the first five pages of the newspaper. She declined to reply. The Press Complaints Commission (PCC) provided me with the Code of Practice for the newspaper industry, which states that:

> All members of the press have a duty to maintain the highest professional and ethical standards. In doing so, they should have regards to the provisions of this Code of Practice and safeguarding the public's right to know.

The Code of Practice states on the subject of accuracy that 'Newspapers and periodicals should take care not to publish inaccurate, misleading or distorted material.' Though it must be said that the Code of Practice also states that 'Newspapers, whilst free to be partisan, should distinguish clearly between comment, conjecture and fact.'

I believe that people with opinions, however distasteful, should be allowed to express them. We live in a country of free speech and bigots have rights too. But we can all try and exercise tolerance. Although newspapers are good at disseminating opinion, I would argue that they are not clear when it comes to the telling the truth. They are obviously in the business of selling papers and people are unlikely to buy papers which oppose their beliefs.

In the early days when the first people with AIDS started dying the British Press were quick to come up with suggestions as to how the HIV virus originated, how it is transmitted and who is most likely to contract it. They said it was a 'gay plague' that also affected 'junkies', (*Sun*, 1983a). This provided the moralists with ammunition to fire at minority groups they already detested. Instead of combating the virus many turned on the gay community, although prejudice against gay men already existed long before the advent of HIV and AIDS (Royal College of Nursing 1994). Solutions to the 'problem' were also offered by the media. The *Sun* reported that 'Loose-living gays should be rounded up and put in ghettoes to stop the spread of the killer disease AIDS' (*Sun*, 1983b). Some papers implied that HIV was God's judgment on homosexuals and people who lead what might be termed as 'immoral lifestyles'. The *Sun* quoted one gay man with AIDS as saying 'I suppose I have paid the penalty for the way I used to live' (*Sun*, 1983a).

Although most people in the western world who are ill with the HIV virus or have AIDS are primarily gay, 'misunderstandings can be seen to have resulted from over-reactions to the description of AIDS as a "gay plague" or a "gay disease". It is perfectly proper to point out that AIDS is not in anyway caused by homosexuality and has no innate ability to identify and target gay men selectively'. However as long-time AIDS survivor Michael Callen has argued, 'It should be possible to get out the message that non-gay people can get AIDS without having to deny or downplay the fact that the overwhelming majority of people with AIDS are gay . . . AIDS is a gay disease because a lot of gay men get AIDS' (King, 1993).

On the origin of the virus, the press have suggested that it may have come from outer space or from the drinking of animal blood during voodoo rituals, although these theories were discredited soon after their sensational appearance (Fallowell 1983). It was clear to most that some of the suggested origins of the virus were so far-fetched that many of them fell at the first hurdle.

The most damaging aspect, apart from the barrage of prejudice against gay men, is the media reporting of transmission routes. The earlier media coverage concentrated on gay lifestyles, intravenous drug use and infection through contaminated blood products. The *Sun* reported that 'Any homosexual who indulges in violent sex play, the complete sex act and exchanges partners with regularity is asking for it. The Government has already requested that such people should not give blood' (*Sun*, 1983a). It must be acknowledged that the same article also stated that, 'Because it is passed through the blood you certainly cannot catch it by shaking hands, drinking out of the same glass, or even from dirty lavatory seats' (*Sun*, 1983a). This was only partly helpful because, although people were getting a more realistic view of how the virus might be transmitted, the emphasis on homosexuals being the only social group at risk lulled many heterosexuals into a false sense of security, putting them at risk and only serving to reinforce the prejudice against gay men.

The government embarked on an educational programme to alert heterosexuals to the risks they may face from HIV when they realized that they were also being infected. The first advertisements featured an iceberg and a tombstone. Nobody really understood what it was all about. I, for one, was walking about for weeks looking up to the sky occasionally to check that a tombstone wasn't about to fall on my head, or even worse an iceberg. As time went by the public education programme did get clearer and the message started to get across. The deaths of Rock Hudson and Freddie Mercury, the involvement of celebrities such as the Princess of Wales and Elizabeth Taylor all helped to contribute towards AIDS awareness.

EROSION OF TRUST

Health care workers generally have an image that is very favourable. They are often seen as sacrificing, dedicated and under-paid. They are thought to be advocates of the general public. In these times of financial uncertainty, where hospitals and smaller practices have become Trusts or Fund holders, health care workers are seen to be on the side of the patient or client. Although working for the management hierarchy, they appear to be as much victims to cuts as are patients. Many members of the public believe that health care workers, particularly nurses, midwives and health visitors are underpaid. Health care workers are the friendly face of the biggest business in the world.

Health care workers are seen as a pillar of stability in the midst of bureaucratic, managerial and financial chaos. They offer hope to the unwell, frail and dying. Britain was renowned for its health care service. Set up by Beveridge at the end of the Second World War it offered new hope for the poor and badly paid. Health care workers were envoys of Beveridge's mission, although even before the advent of the National Health Service, nurses were revered by those injured in wars gone by. The health care profession for many is a safety net for old age and sickness. When the unexpected accident or disaster occurs, health care workers are there to help pick up the pieces long after the police have investigated and the firemen have put the fires out. Caring and rehabilitating, health care workers are the light in a dark world for many and offer hope to those who need it.

The historical development of nursing culminates in the image we have of nurses today. Much credit is given to Florence Nightingale, 'the lady with the lamp'. Her image was one of self-sacrifice with no desire for money or prestige or even recognition. She was a courageous woman who brought nursing out of the dark ages. She was an 'angel of mercy' to those on the battlefields of the Crimea. The 'angel of mercy' image continued into the First World War. 'Nurses were viewed as honorable, moral, spiritual, self-sacrificing, and ritualistic . . . making them a token of exemplary moral purity' (Deloughery *et al.*, 1991). Although this portrayal of Florence Nightingale is probably the most romantic and popular, she is also portrayed as one of the first great feminists, and sometimes as a hard-nosed unpleasant woman. Whatever the case, the conditions she worked under were terrible, and not romantic in the slightest.

According to Deloughery *et al.*, (1991) from 1920 to 1929, 'nursing education regulations were lowered and students were exploited as cheap labour'. Nurses were described as 'faithful, dependent, cooperative, long suffering, and subservient'. The 1930s to the war years made nursing 'acknowledged as a worthy and important profession'. 'Adjectives such as courageous, chivalrous, fearless, reasonable, clear headed, humanitarian, and magnanimous were used to illustrate and portray nurses'. The years after the war up until 1965 saw nurses portrayed as 'maternal, compassionate, unassertive, submissive, and domestic'.

Then things changed dramatically. After 1966 came the sex object image. Every one who has seen the *Carry On* films set in hospitals remembers the wonderfully cheeky Barbara Windsor. Her uniforms were certainly not regulation, often sending her patient's blood pressure through the roof. The same could be said for Bernard Breslaw who was disguised as a nurse in one of the films on a scam to steal contraceptive pills. Despite his hairy legs and great height he had a similar effect on some of the patients as Babs Windsor!

In *MASH*, (an Ameriocan television series and also a movie) Major 'Hot Lips' Houlihan added sex appeal as a surgical nurse to what was in reality a nightmare situation in Vietnam. These images may be fun and quite harmless, but that is not the whole story. Nurses have also been portrayed as sadistic power figures. In the film *One Flew Over the Cuckoos' Nest* a certain Nurse Ratched is 'depicted as a soul-destroying, castrating mother figure. She abused her position as a psychiatric nurse to arrange cruel punishments. In one scene she has a patient lobotomized' (Deloughery *et al.*, 1991). Hattie Jaques, the matron in the *Carry On* films, never lobotomized anyone, but ice baths were the order of the day.

The 1980s brought stories of HIV-infected health care workers to the public's attention. In 1993, the child nurse Beverley Allit was found guilty of murdering patients in her care and in 1994 a male nurse at Great Ormond Street Children's Hospital was found guilty of causing grievous bodily harm to mere babies.

Yet on the whole nurses are thought to be stable, solid people. Nurses and other health care workers are trusted by society, so trusted that the public willingly put their lives into their hands. Because of the general perception of health care workers by the public as being stable, sacrificing model citizens, it is hard for the public to imagine these people being in situations where they might be at risk from contracting HIV because of the social groups HIV is primarily connected with. Many believe that people with HIV have 'let themselves in for it' because they are claimed by a label of one of these groups, e.g. homosexuals. The thought of health care workers with HIV rather tarnishes the angelic, stable, trustworthy image that the health care worker enjoys from the public.

It is not surprising that the media have portrayed HIV-infected health care workers as being a 'high risk' to patients. The image of the health care professional is so incompatible with the morality the media associates with the transmission of HIV that together an explosive reaction occurs and therefore it makes provocative reading and sells newspapers. The subject of HIV-infected health care workers is a story line that is a long way off from becoming boring and dropped from our daily read, because all of us will come into contact with health care workers at some point in our lives, usually more than once. The prospect of the possibility of being infected by one is therefore an issue that affects everyone.

Management and the bureaucratic hierarchy of the health service are considered by many to be so untrustworthy and incompetent that they they are not well placed to counteract the tirade of misinformation. Much of the population does not trust this present government on issues such as the health service, which has undergone many changes since the enviable position it had in the world after Beveridge's plans were implemented. Although the masses might be right to mistrust the powers that be, health care workers themselves are probably best placed to educate the public on the risks they might face from an HIV-infected health care worker.

Unfortunately the trust and faith the public have with health care workers is being gradually eroded by the stories they read about those who are infected continuing to practise in the light of a positive HIV status. This erosion of trust makes the task of educating the public about the negligible risks they face from being cared for by an HIV-infected health care worker difficult.

Health care workers are unfortunately open as anyone else to the same misinformation which might cultivate prejudices. The HIV-positive health care worker therefore might be just as feared by some within the profession as those outside of it. Whilst health care workers are not allowed to discriminate against their patients, they might disapprove of the lifestyle of those they care for. Nevertheless they cannot refuse to care for someone, for discrimination has no place in the health care setting. However, there have been cases of health care workers who suspect a colleague of being infected because of their sexual orientation, who have acted upon the discriminatory views they have on someone's life-style. This highlights the fact that some health care professionals are unaware of the risks of HIV transmission posed by an infected worker and, believing them to be at risk, in their duty to protect patients have informed management of their suspicions based purely on their sexuality or even what someone wears. Many of the problems concerning the subject of HIV are not motivated by ethical or safety issues but by fear.

Any solution to the dilemma posed by HIV-infected health care workers continuing in clinical practice must be a balance between ensuring that procedures are implemented to minimize the actual risk to patients and ensuring that the rights of the health care worker are affected as little as possible. The risks that exist, although negligible, should be put in their true perspective with the risk clearly quantified. It is fear of HIV that makes us overreact, causing an imbalance in the perspective. Efforts should be made to redress the balance.

HIV issues are difficult to balance. Facts are often muddled with opinion, and what is actually an opinion appears to be fact. Whilst it is important that newspapers be partisan they should also make clear what is their opinion and what is actual fact. Opinions based on fear and prejudice and ignorance are the root of the problem. If the facts about HIV-infected health care workers had been reported clearly from the outset then perhaps the fear of such workers would not be so great.

I will conclude this chapter with the words of Richard Ingrams, an esteemed journalist who wrote in the *Observer* after a Glasgow surgeon was found to be HIV-positive at the end of 1994:

Once again enormous publicity has been given to the fact that a hospital surgeon, a specialist of the inner ear, has been diagnosed as being HIV-positive.

All those in positions of authority in the media know by now that there is not the remotest chance that [the doctor] might have passed the virus to one of his patients. Yet this has not stopped the BBC from giving the story the full Shock Horror treatment. As a result, the hospital had to set up a hot line, manned the telephones over Christmas and send out letters to hundreds of the infected doctor's patients offering them coun-selling. Those people who create this scare – as they regularly do – are the very same people who tell us all the time how important it is that the public should be educated in the facts about AIDS and how vital it is to everybody that the disease should not be reported with bias and sensationalism.

The irony is that, as far as doctors are concerned, they themselves are much more at risk from being infected by patients than vice versa – partly because there has been such widespread opposition to any proper testing programme. Yet according to the media's code, Doctor Gives Patient AIDS is a story while Doctor Gets AIDS From Patients is not. (Ingrams 1995)

References

Daily Star (1993) AIDS Doc wins battle to keep his job. 2 September.

Deloughery G., Black, V. L. and Germaine-Warner, C. (1991) Issues in nursing and trends, image of nursing. London: *Mosby Year Book*, p. 378.

Fallowell, D. (1983) AIDS is Here. *The Times* 27 July

Ingrams R. (1995) This watchdog will not bark. *Observer*, 1 January.

King, E. (1993) *Safety in Numbers*. London: Cassell.

Nursing Times (1993) Backward steps.

People (1995) Kiss of death. 15 January.

Pink Paper (1995) 'Arrest' gays Tory stands for Parliament. 20 January.

Rabin, Kenneth (quoted by Mike Cooper) (1989) *CDC AIDS Weekly*, December, 12 (1).

Royal College of Nursing (1994) *The Nursing Care of Lesbians and Gay Men: Issues in Nursing No. 26.*

Sun (1983a), The gay plague that came by skytrain. 11 November.

Sun (1983b) 'Ghetto' plan for killer plague gays. 10 June.

Tavanyar, J. (1992) *The Terrence Higgins Trust HIV/AIDS Book*. London: Harper Collins.

Today (1993) Nurse gets AIDS virus. 23 April.

CHAPTER 7

Comments about HIV-positive health care workers

This chapter illustrates some of the differing views on the continuing practice of HIV-positive health care workers. Research was carried out into the views of Members of Parliament, members of the nursing profession, medical journalists and AIDS activists for comparison. Far more MPs were approached than are represented here, but many failed to respond. I would like to thank all those that replied.

They were all asked whether they thought HIV was compatible with clinical practice. Here are their views.

Daloni Carlisle, Deputy News Editor, *Nursing Times*

HIV and AIDS brings out the worst in some people. They use the medical diagnosis as a respectable cloak in which to wrap their homophobia and racism.

Nursing is no different, and while I've reported on some shining examples of compassionate nurse-led care, I have also covered some appalling incidents where nurses with HIV have seen their careers ruined by careless or malicious breaches of their confidentiality – all at the hands of colleagues. The result? Nurses with HIV tend to keep their antibody status secret.

It is not clear whether people with HIV are welcome in the profession. Officially, the rules say that there is nothing to preclude a person with HIV from completing nurse training. Unofficially, it is a difficult route to take.

The nurses' code of conduct says that all nurses must 'recognize and respect the uniqueness and dignity of each patient and client, and respond to their need for care, irrespective of their ethnic origin, religious beliefs, personal attributes, the nature of their health problems or any other factor'. How can the profession live up to this while it effectively excludes people with HIV from its ranks?

Sir Gerard Vaughan MP

HIV is an infection.

It is not in most cases as infectious as was thought originally.

It can lead to various clinical manifestations.

It is untreatable – although life in some cases can be prolonged.

It is terminal.

It seems to me that it follows from this that it is not compatible with clinical practice and patients should be warned.

There are examples in Italy and America where infection from a professional appears to have taken place.

I appreciate all the problems over confidentiality, and personal problems that may ensue over insurances, mortgages, etc.

I, as a doctor, could not, for example, treat a patient who I know was HIV-positive and not tell his wife, also my patient, that she was at serious risk.

I appreciate the problems over tracing HIV infection but I firmly hold the personal view that it should be a notifiable disease.

It should be a criminal offence for somebody knowing he is infected to be a blood donor.

Nicholas R. Winterton MP

I would simply say that the medical professions themselves are best placed to deal with the sensitive issue of HIV infection amongst medical practitioners.

Clearly there are some disciplines in which HIV infection would be totally incompatible with clinical practices. Alternatively, there are, however, areas of work where contact with a patient is in fact minimal and cross infection is not a real risk in either event. I think that practitioners who are infected have a clear duty to inform their employers immediately, and to seek advice from their professional bodies about their own circumstances.

The Labour Party's consultation document on HIV and AIDS

The rights of health care workers themselves are critical. The likelihood of accidental transmission from patient to health care worker is far greater than vice versa. Doctors, dentists and nursing and midwifery staff must feel protected in their working environment. For the small number of professionals who are HIV-positive, anonymity and appropriate redeployment should be guaranteed in the context of clear and enforced safeguards for patients.

Confronting the reality of HIV and AIDS within the NHS is difficult for those involved. Government must be prepared to advise and to act, in order to ensure that neither patients, nor those who treat them, suffer in dealing with that reality.

Christine Hancock, General Secretary, Royal College of Nursing

HIV-infected health care workers have the right to confidential and sympathetic medical and occupational health advice and support to enable them to continue care for patients safely and effectively. Health care workers who know they are infected with HIV have a responsibility to seek such advice and refrain from engaging in exposure prone procedures to ensure that there is no risk to patients.

The Royal College of Nursing believes that it is necessary to modify or restrict individual's work practices, it is vital that every effort is made to accommodate such changes without loss of status or earnings or any breaches of confidentiality. No applicant for nurse training or a nursing post should be discriminated against purely on the grounds of their known or suspected HIV status.

Peter Brooke MP

Your question could clearly be answered at a number of different levels. Patently somebody engaged in clinical practice should indicate if he or she is HIV-positive, but I think your question was of a different nature, as to whether the law should then preclude him from being engaged in clinical practice. There would be a lay presumption against his practicing but, I do not regard myself as sufficiently expert to know whether that is commanding. What is clear is that a definitive position should be stated by the Department of Health.

Jenny Hope, Medical Correspondent, *Daily Mail*

The Department of Health has produced comprehensive guidelines on HIV-infected health care workers, and I suggest you obtain these.

Carol Harris, Editor, *Therapy Weekly*

I can't understand how some journalists covering the topic can manage to stay so ill-informed. You see some quite interesting and lucid articles, usually in the qualities, but the depth of ignorance shown by some tabloid writers is amazing. The panic over this midwife or that surgeon with HIV seems to me entirely a result of their scaremongering. How many people have ever contracted HIV from an infected health care worker? This question is not even discussed.

Similarly, the issue of contracting HIV from a patient is not considered. And why is HIV an issue when hepatitis is not?

Instead of raising these concerns, health authorities set up help lines for people whose fear is a result of their ignorance, staff resign and witch hunts start to find the 'guilty'. It is almost medieval.

Recently news broke of a dentist who had died of AIDS. One of the tabloids said that he could have infected 1300 people. This was his entire patient list and to draw such a conclusion – it would be funny if it wasn't so sick.

Winston S. Churchill MP

The primary consideration must be the safety of the patient, who must have confidence that procedures are in place to ensure they are not put at risk by the HIV infection of health care workers, including both medical and dental practitioners. All who are likely to come into contact with patients in a way that could lead to the infection of the patient should be asked voluntarily to undergo regular blood tests. The same should apply also in reverse, with patients who are in a potential position to infect health care workers (i.e. during surgical operations) being invited voluntarily to submit a blood test. Special procedures would need to be employed where this is refused, but at least all would be alerted to the need for special care.

John Campbell, Director, UK Coalition of People Living with HIV and AIDS

HIV causes anger, frustration, confusion and so many other mixed emotions that it is often the easiest and most vulnerable populations that become the targets of witch hunts or attacks by those misinformed or ignorant. It has been a recurring story in the AIDS Crisis. Gays, drug users, prostitutes and health care workers have all faced the stigma and prejudice that often accompanies this pandemic. As the world adapts to the reality HIV is here to stay. The need for policies and procedures will need enacting to ensure that all at risk of transmission are protected by coherent and well implemented practices. The NHS has supposedly done this already, therefore I find it appalling that they allow such witch hunts to happen. But it clearly shows the government has failed to inform the population about the ways in which HIV can be transmitted from person to person.

Dr Susan Turnbull, Medical Officer, Communicable Diseases Branch, Department of Health

I confirm that as no general nursing procedures would be regarded as 'exposure prone', i.e. procedures where there is a risk of injury to the nurse such that the open tissues of a patient may be contaminated by the blood of the nurse, then HIV infection should not be regarded as incompatible with either general nurse training, or with general nursing practice.

It should always be stressed that all health care workers must scrupulously follow recommended general infection control measures at all times.

Department of Health spokesperson

So far there has not been a single recorded incident of the virus being passed from health care worker to patient.

CHAPTER 8

Four case histories of HIV-positive health care workers

A positive HIV diagnosis has repercussions for anyone who has a test. Many find themselves faced with the stark reality that they are actually mortal, having never really considered the future prospect of dying which comes to all of us eventually. Those who are HIV-positive may feel cheated by life and that life is no longer worth living. Some even commit suicide. For health care workers, a positive HIV diagnosis can mean the loss of their home (many health care workers, especially students, live in hospital accommodation) and the loss of future career prospects.

The prospect of dealing with the consequences dissuades many people from having the test. As health care workers we are faced with the ethical dilemma of our responsibility to have a test if we believe we have exposed ourselves to the virus, whilst we can see that others who have followed this path have not always received favourable publicity from the press and the reaction of many people is still one based on ignorance.

Any health care workers who reveal themselves to be HIV-positive to others in the health care setting, whether that be the occupational health department or colleagues, face the risk that confidentiality will break down and that their HIV status will become common knowledge. They also may discover for the first time that there are those in the health care setting who are prejudiced and discriminatory towards them.

Anyone who is HIV-positive fears rejection by others, and is therefore careful about whom they need to tell, including family and friends. If HIV-infected health care workers are seen to be rejected by the health care service then obviously that will not encourage disclosure. All health care workers need to know that if they are HIV-positive then all possible efforts will be made to allow them to continue in work, or be reallocated to another area of practice that does not involve exposure-prone procedures if they are still healthy, without loss of home, salary or career status. The UKCC and Department of Health guidelines try to reflect this and there are many cases of health care workers who, having disclosed their status, have found hospital management and occupational health staff to be sympathetic and accommodating.

Discovering that you are HIV-positive is a shock. Most people find that they have to make all sorts of changes to their lives. There are people to tell, often with the risk attached of more hurt and pain, prejudice and fears. Some give up work unnecessarily to live a life of social security benefits. Life assurances that one has paid into for years suddenly become invalid. There is worry over other people they may have infected, and perhaps time spent on wondering who infected them. For most people who are healthy with HIV, it should not interfere with their employment, but for the health care worker an HIV diagnosis may mean significant changes to working environment and practices.

To illustrate the different attitudes an HIV-positive health care worker may face, I shall describe four case histories documenting experiences of HIV-infected health care workers. The cases are completely different, yet all were prompted by a positive diagnosis. The names of the people concerned, along with identifying details, have been changed to preserve anonymity.

These case histories were compiled during several interviews in conjunction with pieces written by the people concerned. I have not transcribed the interviews verbatim, but have used the interviews to construct case studies that are true to each individual's experience. The first part of this book dealt specifically with rights and responsibilities and did not cover in much depth what happens on a personal level to a health care worker when they discover they are HIV-positive. These case studies address issues that are common to people who find themselves to be HIV-positive.

MICHAEL

My name is Michael, I am a gay man living with the HIV virus and I'm twenty-four years-old. It is believed that I contracted the virus when I was seventeen-years-old, though I have only known about my diagnosis for four years. I write to tell my story of how HIV affected my life as a health care worker, in the light of media attention to the subject and the public scare it causes. This is my story . . .

I have been gay for as long as I can remember. I was always the token fag at school. Other people were telling me I was gay long before I accepted it. My years as a teenager ran parallel to the beginnings of the AIDS epidemic. I used to watch the news in fear. Evidence at that time suggested that HIV was contracted through homosexual sex. It was dubbed the Gay Plague. I had always wanted to be a nurse, for as long as I wanted to sleep with men I suppose. I commenced my training at a well known London hospital. I had achieved my first goal in life.

I loved the nurses home, it was an old building full of people, mixed races, religion and all other walks of life. The whole place was painted a cream colour, you know, 'prison magnolia with a hint of institution'. That didn't matter, the rooms were what you made them and with the help of a few posters they could be made to look quite good. You just had to stamp your own identity on them.

Our tuition set was a bit cliquey, there were three different groups within the class and I tried to hover around all of them, making myself as socially available as possible. I was the only gay man in the group, as far as I know. Some of the other students didn't understand my sexuality. Some of them came from far away places and for all I knew it may have been illegal in their native land. The fact that AIDS had many African countries in its grip at this time may have also been on their minds.

The first few months of my training went well. I felt as if I had found my vocation in life.

The patients seemed to like me, as did the qualified staff. The students who had been around a while had a different attitude towards us as first-year students. The hierarchy starts as soon as you enter the profession. At the bottom.

I had been and had the HIV antibody test about eighteen months prior to starting my training. I had never gone back for the result. Fear I suppose, although deep down I knew that I was infected, in the same way that I knew I was gay when I was younger. I pondered about going back for the result. I thought that because of the nature of my work it was my professional duty to do so. The possible consequences of a positive result alarmed me. How would it affect me, and more importantly how would it affect my career? It was a grey area, unknown territory. I had met HIV-positive people who were living their lives as normally as possible. I didn't know any HIV-infected health care workers; how different a positive result would be for one. How different indeed.

There had been, a few months earlier, the case of a doctor who had tested positive. He was exposed by the media, his confidentiality broken and it seemed his career was finished. We never heard of him again. The media offered its thoughts on a solution. Compulsory testing for health care workers. Although it wasn't official policy, I wondered if it was ever carried out secretly. The occupational health department had taken blood from me for other tests. It wouldn't have been too difficult for them to have tested it for the HIV virus or even the sneaky immune profile, so they could have made an educated guess.

A friend of mine had become ill. He had AIDS – and was dying in hospital. I decided to go and visit him. He was unrecognizable when I walked onto the unit and I had difficulty finding him. He was thin and gaunt and very sick. Despite his predicament he was cheerful. We chatted. It was difficult for me at first because of his appearance, but it was good to see that he was in high spirits.

It was this visit that made me again question my own diagnosis. Was I HIV positive? His courage had motivated me. Two days later my friend died.

I caught the tube to the place where I had originally had the test. My feelings were mixed on that journey. I had to stand for some of the way. My legs alternated between solid and liquid. It felt like I had about eight pints of diarrhoea swilling around inside me. On arriving at the clinic, my heart sank. It had closed a few months earlier. There was no way I could have another test and wait a week to find out the result: I had waited eighteen months already. I noticed an open door nearby and walked through it. The room was large, medical records spanned it floor to ceiling. I wondered if mine was amongst them. A man sat at a desk in the centre of the room. I asked him where the records from the clinic had been moved to. He told me that current records were now at a new clinic that had opened at a nearby hospital, about a mile and a half away.

I felt some relief at this, I hopefully wouldn't have to have another test. I made haste to the new clinic. As I walked I wondered what my reaction would be. Part of me already knew that it would be positive. Would I cry? I didn't think I would somehow. Who would I tell? That threw up a lot of questions in my own mind. It scared me more than anything else.

There was no receptionist at the clinic desk when I arrived. I waited and a few other people queued up behind me. I fumbled a little with my fingers, wondering what I was going to say, rehearsing possibilities in my mind. The receptionist returned, she sat down and smiled. I explained to her that I had the HIV test about eighteen months earlier and had finally come for the result. She went to the back of the room. There was a small shelf with a few files on it. My file was there. As she sat back down she opened the file. I stared, stunned. On the page that fell open were the words 'SERO-POSITIVE', stamped in red ink. I became aware of the people standing behind me. My legs turned to liquid again. She shut the file as if nothing had happened and asked me to take a seat, a doctor would be with me shortly. I sat down, all I could feel were my emotions filling my throat. The doctor came out of his room and the receptionist had a brief word with him. I knew that they were talking about me because they kept looking over as she vaguely waved the file at me. The doctor came over and smiled. He shook my hand and we went into his room. I told him that I had come for the result of my HIV test. Without opening the file to look, he said that it was not good news and that I was HIV positive. I could have told him that. It only confirmed my feelings and the receptionist's insensitivity. The doctor examined me. I had no immediate health problems and my health was otherwise all right. He washed his hands and asked me how old I was. 'Nineteen'.

'So young', he whispered back.

On leaving the clinic he asked me what I was going to do.

'Have a drink, a large one', I replied.

I went to the pub for one, that was the intention. I ended up there until closing time. I don't remember talking to many people that night. I must have told them about my day. The morning greeted me with a hangover. In my own mind it wasn't a hangover, I was ill. I got dressed and made my way to the occupational health department and asked to speak to one of the senior nurses. I sat in her office.

This was the right thing to do wasn't it?

She looked shocked. It seemed that they had never had anyone presenting to the department with this diagnosis. The most scandalous thing up until now was probably the odd pregnancy test.

It was decided that I should go on sick leave, until the guidelines for dealing with HIV-positive health care workers were consulted.

My problems had only just begun. Not only did I have my diagnosis to deal with, but also the fact that my career was in question.

Whilst I was off sick I had the time to think about other things. Should I tell my parents? What was I going to say to my boyfriend Tim? He was nearly qualified. He had taken his final exam and was waiting for the result and to everyone that knew him it was a foregone conclusion that he had passed. I met him when I started my training in the hospital. He was well known, and well liked by the senior staff. He was respected by all. Our relationship was also common knowledge and I feared that he would leave me if I confided in him the result, but he had a right to know and so I told him. Tim was his usual caring self. We always had safe sex and he wasn't worried about himself. The occupational health department were interested in talking to him and asked me to ask him to go and see them. They suggested that he have a test himself. I was alarmed at this suggestion. It had taken me eighteen months of thinking about it to convince me of the need to know. That was my right. Now was having a test to be Tim's professional duty?

Tim had the test and it proved to be negative. He duly reported the good news to the occupational health department as they had asked. I now believe that had Tim had a positive test result he would not be working in the profession now.

Initially I trusted the occupational health department. They seemed interested in keeping a close eye on my health. It was suggested that I speak to my senior tutor at the school of nursing. The final decision on this was left up to me and I decided to tell her. After all it was my duty.

My senior tutor seemed as sympathetic as the senior nurse in the occupational health department. It was agreed that we would monitor the situation. Confidentiality was of course assured. At this time only one nurse in the occupational health department knew. My file was under lock and key in her desk. My senior tutor and agreed that two of my other tutors could be told. I stipulated that this was as far as I wanted it to go. It later turned out to be common knowledge.

It turned out that the consultant in the occupational health department had been informed, as had the sister of occupational health; the vice principal had been informed also. The school of nursing and occupational health department started to liaise with each other by phone and letter. In the meantime they were all trying to decipher the UKCC guidelines on HIV-infected health care workers and debating what 'invasive procedures' consisted of.

My opinion of both the school and the department was falling. I didn't feel safe anymore. They were no longer sympathetic. They didn't know what to do with me. I had become a problem.

Six weeks passed by as did my twentieth birthday. It was a quiet one and I wasn't in the mood to celebrate. Tim and I sat in the local pub and had a couple of drinks. That was about it. I felt confused and hurt. It seemed that there were certain things in the hospital that I might not be able to do as I might be a risk to the patients. No one was sure what these certain things might be. I assumed it was assisting in theatre, that sort of thing. Another week passed by, pretty much the same as the week before. That week a few nurses were organizing a party. A Hallowe'en party. My friends encouraged me to go, so I made the effort.

My boyfriend Tim lived in the house where the party was being held. Trying to get into the spirit of things I bought a pumpkin. I hadn't ever hollowed one out before and it was one of those silly ambitions that seem like a good idea at the time. I sat on Tim's bedroom floor with the pumpkin, a newspaper and a knife and got to work. As I cut out the last eye the knife slipped. The cut was so bad that the blood dripped from my fingers. It was the first time I had cut myself since my test result. I was still and just watched for a few moments as the blood dripped onto the newspaper. The knife was still in my other hand. I felt as if I had met the virus. The impact of my result descended on me as the grimacing pumpkin stared back.

The guests started to arrive for the party. Not everyone I knew was there as the late shift at the hospital hadn't finished. Some of the guests seemed to be aware of my diagnosis, they asked me how I was. I retorted that I was feeling fine and then with concerned eyes and sympathetic frown they would ask the same question again. Later a nurse who I only knew by sight came up to me. She asked the very same question, she looked directly into my eyes. Silent for a moment, she drew close to me and whispered in my ear, 'Is there something you want to tell me about your health?' I was lost for words. Who was this woman? I hadn't a clue who she was. She knew more about me than I knew about her. I didn't even know her name.

I wanted to be alone and sat in the corner of the room. The pumpkin stared down at me from a shelf, its eyes and smiling mouth lit by a candle. I surveyed the room through tears. These people had ceased to see me as a colleague; they saw me as a patient.

The next blow of the evening followed shortly. A friend told me that she had heard at a student party a few nights earlier from one of my nurse tutors that I was HIV positive. I couldn't believe it. The particular tutor in question had given us our first lessons on the ethics of confidentiality.

The next day I decided to start fighting to get control of my life back. With the help of my friend and a few other witnesses to the event I went to see my senior nurse tutor. I think she felt embarrassed because it looked as though the leak came from the school. I had specifically asked that my confidentiality was safe, but I was getting used to the fact that confidentiality for staff was a different kettle of fish to that we afford our patients.

A meeting was arranged for me to see the vice-principal. He apologized for the actions of the tutor concerned and informed me that the tutor had left the school of nursing and had gone to work for another health authority. It was briefly mentioned that if I wanted, I could approach the UKCC to follow up disciplinary procedure. My colleagues who had witnessed this breach of confidentiality were not so keen to help me now. I can understand this, their final exams were approaching. Anyhow I was getting used to people pledging support and then taking it away.

I could see my career trickling down the drain. Nobody would commit themselves to helping me and no one would dream of giving me anything in writing. My mental and physical health were suffering from the stress. I isolated myself from my friends and spent a lot of time on my own in my room.

One morning I heard a key in the door. It was one of the porters from the nurses' home and two of my friends. They seemed relieved to see me as I looked over the top of the sheets. They must have felt a bit foolish as they explained to me that they thought I was dead and that they had the door opened to make sure I was, or wasn't as the case may be. I agreed to meet them down in the canteen after I had got dressed. I hadn't been eating very well and my weight had dropped slightly. To those who knew me it was noticeable.

I sat with my friends over tea and buns. The conversation was strained. Eventually they went back to work and I was left on my own whilst the cleaners did their bit. I felt detached from everything around me and I began to wonder what I was. Did I work there or was I a patient? There was no happy medium. I was trapped between the two. Where did I belong?

I went back to my room and as I approached the door I noticed something familiar. Someone had thoughtfully put a bio-hazard sticker on my door whilst I was downstairs at the canteen. As I peeled it off with my fingernails one of my classmates walked into the toilet opposite my room. She was carrying a plastic bag. She ignored me. I later found out that the bag was to protect her from HIV whilst using the toilet! People were frightened of me.

In the week that followed the occupational health department let me go back to the school to prepare for the next ward which was care of the elderly. I had missed most of the last block, which had been surgical. I wondered if the school would put me back a set so that I could do the surgical block again. They didn't think that this was a good idea. I continued with care of the elderly. I sat in on the first few lessons. My confidence was in a worse state than I thought. I couldn't concentrate. Was there any point in me being there at all? I asked to be excused and was allowed to go home. Back at home I cried for the first time since I had received my HIV diagnosis.

I wrote in my diary for much of the time during this period. It is still painful for me to go back through and read the entries. I decided that Tim and I should not continue with our relationship. He had been good to me, but if they were going to destroy me I wasn't going to take him with me. I realized that the destruction of my career was imminent and I had to try and prepare for it as best as I could. The biggest problems were the basics. My room at the nurses' home was connected to the job, so presumably I would have to find somewhere else to live. I applied to the council for housing. The situation was deteriorating rapidly and I feared becoming homeless.

I spoke to the consultant who was looking after me. He told me that the occupational health department consultant thought that my training should be discontinued. He had disagreed with this and had written a letter to him. My consultant couldn't see any real reason why I shouldn't be allowed to continue working. There was a glimmer of hope. Perhaps I was not going to be jobless, homeless and without the relationship I wanted, but that was not to be the case. The occupational health department consultant wrote back. His reasons for me not being able to work were thus: As a student nurse I could not be considered competent enough to be able to carry out an invasive procedure safely. I therefore would not be able to carry out any invasive procedure at all. This would include injections, suture removal, etc. There was also a problem with insurance. Should I infect a patient with the HIV virus, who would be responsible? At the end of the day the occupational health department are responsible for the state of your health. If they deem that you are not safe to work, that is the last word. It was out of my consultant's hands. I asked to see the correspondence that had been floating around. After all it was my career in the balance, but I was denied access. I was totally in the dark.

My biggest problem was that nobody understood what the UKCC policy on HIV-infected health care workers meant. The policy was open to whoever interprets it, in my case a doctor near enough retirement age. My consultant was sceptical that this doctor had any knowledge of the HIV virus at all and had even suggested that the Occupational Health Department consultant attend one of his seminars.

Time lumbered on. I spent a few weeks working on the care of the elderly unit. I suppose I was fortunate that I was on that particular block at the time. Very few 'invasive procedures' there! The nature of work and the severity of dementia on this ward finished me off. Most people found this unit stressful and many people would drop out of the course at this point. The ward, compounded with my HIV status and the problems that brought, broke my spirit. I could go on no longer. There was no one I could talk to in confidence. I was beaten.

(*In April 1991, almost a year to the day that Michael had started the course, he resigned from RGN training.*)

ROBERT

London had always appealed to me, so when I qualified as a nurse I moved down to London. I really wanted to do my nurse training there, but circumstances at home stopped me from going so I stayed near my home town in Scotland and pursued my career there. When I finally got to London I found the life that I always had wanted. I knew I was gay from a very early age and where I used to live in Scotland there was nothing in the way of clubs or bars that would cater for me. You can imagine my delight when I arrived in London to find that there were bars all over the place and a well established gay scene.

I knew a little about HIV and AIDS before I came to London. The knowledge that I had was not gleaned from the classroom or the ward environment, but from a national gay magazine that I subscribed to. There were often articles relating to the subject, mainly talking about transmission routes. I was also aware of what the national press were saying about HIV and AIDS. It was the 'gay plague' as far as they were concerned and their crusade against people like me was in full swing. Up here in Scotland there was a lot of hostility towards gay people anyway. I knew only two other gay people there, they were a lot older than me and were a couple. They lived in a small village, in a big house. They were not Scottish, but had come from England seeking a large property for a small price. Obviously any new people in a village up there stand out. Everyone knew everyone else and if anyone new came along one found you got to know them quickly. I suppose these guys lived what I would call an idyllic lifestyle. They had come up to Scotland by choice. I wanted to get out.

I must admit I was not really sure of the routes of transmission of HIV and it was only when I started working in a London hospital that I started to learn about it. I have many gay friends nowadays and as the years have gone by most gay people can probably cite a friend who has died from AIDS or who has the virus. Some of them if you asked them may even mention my name.

I tested HIV positive about two years ago. It was a bit of a surprise because I have had regular HIV tests and they had all been negative up until then. Many of my friends are HIV positive and are getting on with their lives. It was good to be able to talk to them about how the virus might affect me. They were able to help me understand most things about how my life might change, except my career; of this they had no knowledge. I was a bit apprehensive about telling anyone at first. I had seen much of the media coverage on doctors and nurses who had been fired, forced to resign or just plain hounded by the tabloid press.

In the first instance I spoke to someone I trusted, a nurse on the AIDS unit at our hospital. He told me that there were guidelines on how to handle a situation like this. He also told me that there were a few other HIV positive nurses who worked at the hospital having followed the guidelines and were happy about the way that they were treated.

My friend said to me that I had a duty to my patients and myself to alert the occupational health department. He told me that I might be putting myself at risk if I worked in areas of the hospital where I might contract other infections. I knew he was right, but I wanted to think about it at first. It seemed a big step to take. I took a couple of days off sick and went to stay with a friend in Brighton. I had much to think about on that visit to Brighton. Usually I had a great time in the pubs and clubs, but this time I just sat on the beach and looked out to the sea.

I was frightened about what my friend had told me. He seemed quite pushy about the idea about me telling the hospital. I know that there were other people who worked there who were supposedly HIV positive, but that didn't stop me from feeling the way that I did.

I watched the waves creep up onto the beach and I felt comforted by the fact that I was alone on the beach. No one could hear my thoughts there, probably a good job too, as the quiet around me was drowned out by the sound of my own head asking questions. Questions about my career, my home, my parents, in essence everything. One question followed by another. I felt at the same time probably all the other things that one would feel if discovering they were HIV-positive. I can only speak for myself, but I was scared. I had seen slides of people covered in Karposi's Sarcoma; they were traumatic enough without thinking about it happening to you. That's the other thing; I had always thought that this sort of thing only ever happened to other people. I had been careful, or at least I thought I had. My mind kept on swinging to who could have infected me, where did I meet them and what did we do that led to this?

Then more sinister thoughts followed. I pondered over the possibility that someone may have done this to me on purpose. I had read the occasional story in the press about young guys who have the attitude that if they've got it then why shouldn't everyone else. A sick feeling in the pit of my stomach would surge out of feelings I was having for other thoughts and with it came the question, had I infected anyone else? Could I infect anyone else?

I thought again about what my friend on the AIDS unit had told me. I knew deep down that I should tell someone, but I was so worried about the consequences. I suppose it was because of the fact that other nurses at the hospital that I worked at had been treated so well, that encouraged me to come forward. Had I not been sure at all of the consequences, I probably would have kept it a secret.

On my return to London I reported in to the occupational health department. I spoke initially to the nurse on duty. I must say she was a little shocked and seemed in a bit of a quandary as to what to do with me. She asked me if she could talk to the occupational health physician about my situation. It was at this point that I wondered if I had done the right thing. Some of the feelings I had on the beach in Brighton looking out to the sea came back. I comforted myself with the thought that in the great scheme of things it didn't really matter anyhow and I had come this far, perhaps it was better for me to show willing. It felt like my career was in the balance for more than a moment. I waited in an adjoining office whilst the nurse I had spoken to went to find the doctor and I didn't have to wait long for both of them to return. The doctor came in, the first thing he did was shake my hand. The doctor sat down and asked the nurse to leave us. We talked about how I found out about my diagnosis and how I felt in myself, how did I feel in myself at this juncture in time?

On the one hand I clearly felt that there was no turning back, at least I didn't have to worry about telling them anymore. Obviously the consequences of telling them were worrying me and I kept on wondering how genuine was this doctor's concern?

I truly believe now that his concern really helped, his showing interest in my situation. He assured me that I was not the first person he had met who was HIV positive in the hospital and really put me at my ease. At least he seemed to know what he was doing. He asked many questions about my work and what my duties were. The doctor wanted to know what aspects there were to my work and what sort of path my work took. He continued to ask me questions for a while and I was much relieved when he told me that if I was healthy there was no reason why I could not continue to work, so long as I didn't carry out exposure-prone procedures. He wanted to find out more about my work, so he could advise me on any changes in my work practice, if need be. He explained that I would need to attend the occupational health department to be monitored from time to time and also suggested that I seek advice from my own HIV specialist to find out what risk I was at, if any, from infectious diseases on the ward to myself.

I was much more relaxed and comfortable having talked to the doctor. Having read the coverage in the press about other health care workers who had been found to be HIV-positive and what had happened to them I was apprehensive about what would happen to me. I feel secure in the knowledge that the occupational health department at the hospital where I work had done its research. It is only because they had a strategy for dealing with this scenario that things, for me, went smoothly. It seems I am not the only one at the hospital who is nursing whilst being HIV-positive.

I suppose I am fortunate living in London. There is a high concentration of people who are positive here and there is a clinic attached to the hospital that deals specifically with HIV. I have a friend in Manchester who is still too afraid to disclose his diagnosis. Until health care workers feel safe enough to disclose their HIV status to their employers there will be many who will keep it secret. For me things turned out well and I hope that my story will encourage others to come forward, for their own health's sake. And what of my life now?

Well, I am still working and so far, with fingers crossed, I am still healthy. I don't bandy about my HIV diagnosis because there are many people, even within this profession, who still do not understand. I am so grateful to the occupational health doctor; if he had over-reacted or was not in receipt of the facts things could have been a lot different.

I also wonder what sort reaction I would have got had I been back home. The local hospital where I live is very small and the occupational health department is attached to a larger hospital. Even though it is large, I really don't believe I would have got the same response from them. I thank my lucky stars that there were others who laid the path before me at the hospital that I work at and that they had some sort of local policy and strategy for dealing with the situation of an HIV-infected health care worker. I think otherwise my story may have had a very different outcome.

KAREN

My name is Karen. Yes, girls get it too! I would rather not say how I contracted the virus, I hope you don't mind. It isn't really relevant, after all HIV is HIV and that is that. I don't believe that it matters how one is infected. I get sick and tired of people asking me how it happened. I feel that if they knew they might judge me or see me in a different light. That is only one side of the coin. The other side is that when someone knows that you are HIV positive or have AIDS then they sometimes can't see beyond the disease and you almost cease to be seen as a person anymore, and in some people's eyes they may see you as dead already. I know that is how many people feel on diagnosis. That was certainly the way that I felt, though today I do feel differently. I have had the virus for many years. Initially on finding out I climbed into bed for about three weeks, just waiting to die. Then I got bored and got up and started to face the fact the HIV had become a factor in my life.

I have been a general nurse for six years at a hospital in the north of the country. I have been aware I was HIV positive for five years. I didn't tell anyone when I found out I was HIV positive and kept it a secret from everyone for almost three years. I don't know how I managed to keep it to myself for so long. Like I said, I had started to face the fact that I was HIV positive myself, but I couldn't bring myself to tell anyone. For five years I have felt like a fraud in my profession, working with people who were ill and knowing that I had a disease that one day may well kill me. It is quite an achievement when I think about it that I managed to keep it secret for so long. I know that the government and the UKCC require that I should have told someone on diagnosis, but I just couldn't. I was convinced that if anyone found out I would lose my job. That would have been a double blow for me. When one finds out that they are HIV-positive a grieving process starts to take place. It can be a very personal thing, although some people like to have someone close, like a counsellor that they can talk to, and work it out that way. It is no easy feat coming to terms with an HIV-positive diagnosis. I don't feel that is something that you ever accept, but something that one can learn to deal with on a daily basis and adapt to.

I often wonder if it would be easier to be living with something like leukaemia. It doesn't seem to carry the same baggage as having HIV. Perhaps there are no feelings of guilt or remorse for past behaviour and people might treat you in a different way, rather than judging you on how you contracted the virus in the first place. I must admit there were many times that I felt frightened and because of this fear I was not actively seeking any medical help. This on the one hand was a good way of dealing with it initially, although I stress that everyone is different and have their own ways of dealing with and there is no right or wrong way of doing that. However, taking such a stance did have ramifications for my health in the future.

I know now that perhaps my first bout of PCP, an AIDS-related pneumonia, may have been avoided if I had been monitored. Had I been monitored the clinic would have known that my T4 cell count was low and given me prophylaxis treatment to lessen the possibility of developing PCP. I didn't know about this, in fact HIV was a disease I knew very little about. I had avoided the study days as I didn't want to sit there squirming, wondering what they would do if they knew about me. Once again, just another way of dealing with something that I didn't really want to look at.

Perhaps it wasn't so much a case of keeping my HIV status a secret for five years but more a case of being in denial. Even so, that did not stop those dark thoughts from nagging in the back of my head. I would drink to quash those thoughts and as time went by I found myself consuming huge amounts of alcohol and unable to stop. What would my friends think of me if they knew? I wondered if they would see me as a failure as a nurse, HIV-positive and an alcoholic; when I think back it was all so totally insane. I felt very isolated by the fact that I had these secrets and didn't feel I could tell anyone.

You may be asking yourself what stopped me from sharing those secrets with anyone else. The answer is very simple. I was frightened. Frightened by what I heard other people saying about HIV and those who were positive. I know that nurses are supposed to be at the very least tolerant, but often they are not. They are human beings, after all. It was the discrimination and reaction to people with HIV and AIDS that stopped me from seeking help. It is such a dreadful thing that sometimes those working in the profession have such a negative attitude towards people who are ill and need supporting. Many health care workers see the person with the virus as the enemy and not the virus itself.

My painful secret ended one day whilst at work, having just finished a run of nights I came home exhausted and feeling breathless. I thought it might be because I smoke too much. I had been trying to give up on and off without much success. I had organized five days off before I started on my next run of nights and I went to bed with my hot water bottle feeling a bit sorry for myself. I used to worry myself silly whenever I got a cold or any other symptoms and the thought that it might be serious always lurked in the back of my head.

The next morning when I woke up I could hardly move. There was a pain in the left side of my chest that got worse whenever I breathed in. I crawled out of bed and looked at myself in the mirror. I certainly didn't look very well. It was at that point I finally broke down. I had to tell someone, I couldn't keep it a secret any more.

I went to see my GP. I hadn't seen a doctor since my HIV diagnosis, well not for HIV related stuff anyway. I told her I was HIV positive and she told me to go to casualty straight away. She didn't want to deal with me herself, she said it was because she didn't know that much about the virus and that the hospital would be better placed to deal with me. Oh God, I thought, people knew me at the hospital. But the pain was so bad and I felt so ill that it seemed I had little choice. It was time for me to stop pretending and make that transition from a health care worker to a patient. The doctor rang ahead and told them there was an HIV positive woman coming to casualty and could they see me straight away? I got a taxi from the doctor's surgery to the hospital where I worked. I sobbed all of the way there. There were a few surprised faces in casualty when the HIV woman who presented herself there was me and so ended my five-year secret.

I felt more relief than anything because I was finally getting help and that the secret was out. I also felt my conscience relax about working with an HIV diagnosis. The doctors in the casualty diagnosed me with PCP, an AIDS-related pneumonia. I was admitted to the HIV unit where they treated me for it. It was certainly a strange experience being the patient. I was used to being on the other side of the bed. It took about two weeks for me to get better on an IV drip that eventually knocked the PCP on the head. Whilst on the ward, I was told that had the HIV specialist known, they could have put me on prophylactic treatment that may have perhaps protected me against PCP. Things have moved on considerably in terms of HIV treatment; ten years ago people were dying of PCP and it was untreatable. Today they can cure it, indeed some people can survive several bouts of it. I am grateful for that. I didn't know that there was some hope and help that I could have been given if only the right people knew about my HIV status.

In retrospect I should have sought help sooner. I know now I was foolish to keep it a secret for so long. I feared that if I had said anything I may have lost my job, and who knows, I may well have lost it. I'm sure it is the same for anyone in any profession. Fear of being unable to pay the mortgage and other financial pressures stop many from acting appropriately when they find themselves ill.

You may have gathered that I am not nursing anymore; usually I am a patient where I used to work. Like I said, it is certainly a strange feeling being a patient, being on the other side for so many years. I am learning to adapt to my disease and on a daily basis I try and accept that sometimes I may be ill and unable to do things that I used to do. It is not all gloom and doom, though; I have had AIDS for a few years now and I am still here.

My last word on the subject is that I would not advise anyone to do as I did. Seek help. There is hope and it is possible to live with HIV and AIDS.

ANTHONY

My name is Anthony and I used to be a midwife. There are quite a few of us these days, it is quite acceptable for a man to be a midwife. I come from and worked in the north of England. There is a good gay scene up here, almost as busy as London. I would go for a regular HIV test every six months or thereabouts. I always tried to practise safe sex, but there were occasions when I didn't. I know that sounds a bit senseless, but sometimes taking a risk was half the fun. Sex for me was often a spontaneous act and I didn't like those sexual experiences that were similar to a scripted or choreographed event, and occasionally the condoms would go out of the window. This would usually happen more if I had been drinking. I often wonder if my drinking behaviour was more to blame than the actual act of sex itself.

It was on one of those occasions when I went for my routine six-monthly HIV test that I eventually tested positive. I would always feel on one of those days the relief when they told me that I was not infected and I would say to myself, 'Anthony, try and stay that way.' Alas, on this occasion I couldn't say that to myself because this time I was infected.

I felt as if I was completely to blame. I knew that I had tested negative for HIV several occasions before and I made the assumption wrongly that it would be the same again. I never expected that I would get a positive result. I had no hesitation in telling the occupational health department that I was HIV positive. I felt I had to because of the nature of the work I was involved in. Being a midwife my hands are not always visible when working. Indeed, when involved in episiotomy I am using sharp instruments whilst my hands are not visible. When I went to the occupational health department they did react quite a bit. There was a bit of a panic and I got the feeling that they were unsure of what to do with me. It was decided that, as I had been involved in exposure-prone procedures, the health authority would conduct a look-back exercise to make sure no one had been infected by me in the course of my duty, although the risk I was told was very small. I was apprehensive at first and against the idea completely for fear of publicity and my confidentiality being broken. The health authority assured me that every effort would be made to protect my confidentiality, although they would have to hold a press conference as part of the look-back procedure.

The press conference was well attended and journalists pumped for more details as to my identity. They were not interested in how small the risk was. They wanted to speak to me. I believe that the health authority did their best in the circumstances, and it seemed initially that they had succeeded in protecting my confidentiality. That was until a television crew turned up on my mother's doorstep. She didn't know I was gay, let alone HIV positive, and that was the way she found out, on her doorstep. On television my mother looked confused and all she could say was that I had been delivering babies only the weekend before. Someone had betrayed my confidentiality and I have my suspicions as to who told the press.

I had some explaining to do and I told my mother everything. I believe that my parents could have coped better if my plight hadn't been made public. I am no longer practising as a nurse and I feel very bitter about what happened. I believe that the health authority completely overreacted and as a result I am no longer working. I am healthy at the moment and could easily work, but now I am unemployable, no one wants someone who is HIV-positive. I am not sure if that is the same all over the country, but it certainly is the case up here in the north of England.

Every time I see another story in the newspaper it brings up a lot of anger. There should be stricter controls on the media to report the facts. My life will never be the same. In small towns such as the one I live in news travels quickly. Some of my mother's friends don't call her any more and my father won't speak to me. I haven't been home whilst he is there since, as he won't have me in the house. He says I have disgraced the family name.

I would never knowingly hurt another person. I thought that by disclosing my HIV status I was doing the right thing. It seems, however, that I was stripped of my rights as soon as I became HIV positive. Perhaps I should never have gone for those regular HIV tests. I will probably be healthy for many more years; perhaps I should have left it until later. Had I known that this would be the outcome I would have thought twice about having the test in the first place. Of course it has affected my life in many other ways also.

When are people going to understand that it is not those with the virus that is the problem – it is the virus itself. We need to be concentrating on that aspect. In the meantime I have become a social enemy.

CHAPTER 9

Conclusion

The Department of Health state that as of June 1995 there are over 25,000 known HIV-infected individuals in the United Kingdom to date. The actual figure can only be estimated. Although HIV prevention methods are finally having some sort of effect, people continue to be infected. Many of them will die of AIDS leaving behind partners, family, friends and children. I can't comprehend a tragedy so vast. I too may well die of this disease and become one of those statistics mentioned in this book – my biggest wish is that people are not frightened of me.

(Paul Mayho)

The case of the HIV-infected health care worker can have many outcomes and naturally all could not be presented here. However, this chapter reiterates the dilemma of the health care worker with a quantification of risk. It also looks at the problems and failures we have had in educating the population in relation to the HIV-infected health care worker and where those problems have originated from. My final message to the reader could be deemed as idealistic, but I hope that what I have written presents a hope for a future in the health care profession that is tolerable and safe for everyone who uses it and works in it alike.

The fear of HIV-infected health care workers is way out of proportion to the risk, and if every health care worker with HIV were dismissed it would have little impact on the epidemic. Although the risks may appear frightening, discriminating against health care professionals is not conducive to any long-term HIV-prevention strategy.

There is not one case of HIV being transmitted by a health care worker to a patient in Britain to date, though we know that the case of the Florida dentist David Acer raises questions about this statement on a worldwide level. It is evident from DNA strand testing that the virus carried by five of his clients had nearly the same DNA sequence as Acer's virus. This would suggest that health care worker to patient transmission had occurred, though the actual mode of transmission is unknown and we can only surmise from the limited data available what had happened.

When Kimberly Bergalis, one of Acer's infected patients, gave a fifteen-second testimony just before her death calling for the mandatory testing and dismissal of HIV-infected health care workers it was termed by one long-time observer of the AIDS epidemic as 'political dynamite' and by another as being 'the most dangerous moment in the history of the epidemic' (Berke 1991). And so the possibility of being infected by an HIV-infected health care worker permeated the public conscience.

The current statistical data and research carried out into the risks of HIV transmission from infected health care workers to a patient suggest that the risk is only 'potential' (Department of Health 1994). However, a potential risk is still a risk, no matter how small it is, and as health care workers we have a professional duty to our patients to ensure that the risk remains only potential. In carrying out this duty it is up to every individual health care worker to consider their moral, ethical and legal responsibility to the patient. This must, however, be balanced with the actual risk. Even if HIV transmission from a patient is an 'identifiable risk' or 'potential', it should be remembered that being hit by a speeding police car, being blown up at a petrol station or dying on the surgeon's table are also 'identifiable risks' and therefore 'potential'. Indeed people are killed and injured in car accidents every day, yet we may be more worried about the nuclear reactor next door going bang and killing us that way. Why is this? Because there is more chance of being killed in a car accident; if nuclear reactors went bang every day I am sure they would all be decommissioned and pulled down. I use this analogy to help the reader see that although the risk of transmission from an HIV-infected health care worker exists, it is however minuscule and the public reaction to those infected in the health care profession and the media coverage the subject has received are out of proportion to the risk. People are not being infected on a daily basis by health care workers, indeed since the emergence of the epidemic nearly 15 fifteen years ago the CDC in Atlanta would commit themselves only to five people known to be infected in this way worldwide.

If this is so, then the Department of Health's reaction and that of the UKCC are out of all proportion to the risk. By suggesting that health care workers who are HIV-positive are not considered to be safe enough to carry out exposure-prone procedures they have only thrown more fuel on the fire of the public's fears. This leads people who do not engage in risk activities to believe that a large number of individuals (the NHS is the biggest employer in the country) could kill them. Although the Department of Health and the UKCC have tried to address this, nice explanations of 'exposure-prone procedures' are lost upon the public, who consider only the fact that there is a risk rather than quantifying it and comparing it to other risks, particularly other risks in the health care setting. Glantz, Mariner and Annas (1992) suggest that it is the newness of the threat that causes the problem. 'When it comes to risks, familiarity often breeds acceptance.' Slovic (1987) says that 'Risks also tend to be tolerated in direct proportion to the degree to which they are voluntarily accepted by their victims.' Finally on this subject is the 'horror' element: the more horrid the death, the more frightening it becomes. 'If people think of death at all, they are more likely to consider how they do not want to die than how they probably will' (Glantz et al., 1992).

In practice, one's individual responsibility to have an HIV test if one believes they are infected, stated as a professional responsibility in the Department of Health's and UKCC's guidelines, is overshadowed by the possible consequences of a positive result and ultimately is not an encouragement to health care workers to fulfil that responsibility. Restriction from exposure-prone procedures is confined to known HIV-infected health care workers, which is reason for many not to be tested in the first place.

It should be remembered, as stated in the Department of Health guidelines, that all practitioners and all patients pose a potential infection risk whatever the infection may be and all health care workers should observe universal precautions and work to the guidelines of good clinical practice. This book has reiterated the importance of the stringent use and practice of universal precautions and the duty of health care workers to ensure the safety of their patients at all times, and HIV is one motivation to practise them. The Department of Health clearly state that they should always be observed and diligently followed (Department of Health 1994).

Just because a health care worker is known to be HIV-positive is no reason to believe that they cannot or will not carry out universal precautions properly. Indeed, those who are aware of their HIV-positivity in my experience are very conscientious of any potential risk they may pose to others and are more aware of how important it is to maintain the highest standards of infection control and quality care. If there is a problem, it may lie with those who are unaware of their status, which, incidentally, is most of the health care profession, who for one reason or another may practise universal precautions only with those they believe are a risk.

Whilst there are those who are unaware of their HIV status, and there must be many who are HIV-positive, it can be assumed that the risk of transmission of HIV from a health care worker to a patient during clinical procedure, and even exposure-prone procedures, is so small as to be negligible since no one has been found to be infected in Britain in this way. This would also suggest that universal precautions in this country are sufficient to prevent cross infection of the virus. It should, however, be borne in mind that it is also unlikely that a patient would be notified, and if appropriate given the opportunity to have an HIV tests if the health care worker concerned was not known to be HIV-positive.

On the question of responsibility to have an HIV test if one believes oneself to be infected, and this responsibility being upon the individual rather than enforced by mandatory testing, here the recommendations of the Department of Health and the UKCC are inconsistent. 'They state that health care workers should know whether they are infected with HIV. The only way to enforce such a recommendation would be by testing, yet mandatory testing was specifically rejected. In support of its position against mandatory testing, the CDC argued that the current assessment of the risk of transmission does not support the "diversion of resources that would be required to implement such a mandatory testing program" (Center for Disease Control 1991). However, if all health care practitioners who perform exposure prone procedures should know their HIV antibody status, the resources required to comply with this recommendation would be no different from the resources required for mandatory testing.' (Glantz et al., 1992).

If the risk posed by HIV-infected health care workers was so great as to warrant stopping them all from carrying out exposure-prone procedures, then surely it is wrong to rely on health care workers to come forward voluntarily, and if the interests of public safety should come first then all HIV-infected health care workers should be located. It is not enough just to remove a health care worker from an area of practice. This has virtually no effect on HIV transmission. What should be done, instead of discriminating against those known to be HIV-infected, is that efforts should be made to ensure that all health care workers practise universal precautions with all patients. The public also need to know that these precautions are sufficient to prevent transmission of the virus. The need to know a health care worker's HIV status is not an infection control measure.

It should also be remembered that health care workers all over the world face the more realistic potential of being infected by a patient with HIV, and this is another good reason for practising universal precautions, although, universal precautions may not in themselves be adequate to totally eliminate the risk of HIV transmission from a patient. The worldwide statistic as of May 1995 for occupationally acquired HIV infection was 214. The UK statistics show four cases documented after a specific occupational exposure and seven other possibly occupationally acquired infections. The USA statistics are the largest at 134 and the rest of the world stands at 69 (PHLS, 1995). Such statistics in my opinion are unbalanced, for it should be remembered that these statistics are recorded occupational transmissions and that there are many health care workers who have not been tested for HIV after an occupational exposure, particularly in the poorer countries of the world.

The fact that HIV-infected health care workers are not a real risk to patients should be reflected in any future guidance or public education campaign.

Since the risks of HIV transmission in the clinical setting is a problem that does not really exist, the reaction of the press in Britain can only be described as a hysterical preoccupation and journalists capitalizing on the fears of the public. The media portrayal of HIV-infected health care workers discussed in chapter six could have been expanded with many more examples, but many newspapers were not prepared to allow themselves to be criticized and refused to allow reproduction of their work.

Dealing with the media has been the most frustrating element I have encountered in writing this book. I have found most of the press and their editors and journalists unhelpful and unprepared to change their arguments concerning the continuation of practice of an HIV-infected health care worker. Journalists are expected to follow their own set of guidelines on AIDS reporting. Most of the time they are ignored and newspapers publish what they want to anyway. In this respect the British press are not really serving the interests of society and the irresponsible reporting of many journalists has only served to generate an unnecessary fear amongst the general public.

Using the popular media for health education purposes in my opinion has failed or at the very least has been problematic and not conducive to the aim. The reason for this is that HIV mainly affects social groups which are deemed undesirable by the press, who are more interested in the morality of transmission than in the clinical reality of the disease. Health care workers, being in a trusted and revered position, make good targets for journalists. It shocks some of the population to think that those they revere so much must have put themselves in situations to become infected in the first place.

It has to be said that we have learnt much within the health care profession because of the emergence and effects of HIV. One could say that some good has come out of it, but at what a cost. The history books may say in the future of HIV, that it was a considerable milestone in the development of nursing practices and care of the terminally ill. Much has been learnt already and much is to be learnt in the future.

As health care workers we must remember that we are trusted servants of the public. It is clear that we must abide by the UKCC's Code of Professional Conduct, which states:

Each registered nurse, midwife and health visitor shall act, at all times, in such a manner as to:
• Safeguard and promote the interests of individual patients and clients;

- Serve the interests of society;
- Justify public trust and confidence; and
- Uphold and enhance the good standing and reputation of the professions.
  (UKCC 1991)

The expectations of the health care worker can be condensed into these four points, whether HIV-positive or not. It is also expected of the health care worker to 'maintain and improve [your] professional knowledge and competence' (UKCC 1991). It is hoped that the future will see the introduction of compulsory AIDS awareness and study for all health care workers. Only through knowledge of HIV can we fight discrimination. In not doing so we fail our obligation to the public as health educators.

We all pride ourselves as health care professionals on the way we care for our patients and spend our training and professional lives improving our standards of care and understanding of the problems our society faces today. However, despite the profession's solidly based foundations, individual bricks may periodically loosen from their mortar, causing an imbalance and at times a collapse in the building framework. Individual health care workers discover that whilst their colleagues devote much time and commitment to their patients there seems to be very little care for fellow colleagues. Indeed, 'individual needs count less than the corporate needs.' (Tschudin 1992). HIV is here for the foreseeable future. Whilst efforts to treat the effects of HIV are moving forward considerably, vaccination and cure are both years away. Much money is being ploughed into research, but, alas, not enough, and too late for many with the virus. In the meantime our efforts as health care workers should be directed towards the care of those with the virus and we should try to promote a climate that is non-discriminatory and humane towards those affected. As health care workers we have a vital role to play, and whether infected or not, all can contribute in some way to our society. Perhaps more importantly, the future will see a profession develop where there is more unity and humility amongst its workers and managers.

The risk of HIV transmission should be a socially accepted risk. People using the health care service face much higher risks from other aspects of health care such as anaesthesia and surgery. These are considered to be socially accepted risks. In comparison to those risks HIV transmission from a health care worker to a patient should not have to be even a consideration if everyone is doing what they are supposed to. In this way we can fulfil the requirements of our specific codes of conduct.

If health care workers with HIV are considered to be such a risk, 'then eyeglass wearing bus drivers are outside the protection of the law because if their glasses fall off they may go over a cliff and kill a bus load of people' (Glantz, Mariner and Annas 1992).

References

Berke, R. L. (1991) AIDS battle reverting to 'Us against them'. *New York Times*, 6 October.

CDC (Center for Disease Control) (1991) Revised recommendations for preventing transmission of Human Immunodeficiency virus and Hepatitis B to patients during invasive procedures. 27 November, Atlanta, Ga. (unpublished draft).

Department of Health (1994) *AIDS/HIV Infected Health Care Workers – Guidance on the Management of HIV Infected Health Care Workers*, London: HMSO.

Department of Health (1995) Reported occupationally acquired HIV infections in health care workers. Photocopied sheet, May. Also available from the Public Health Laboratory Service.

Glantz, Leonard H., Marriner, Wendy K. and Annas, George J. (1992) Risky business: setting public policy for HIV infected health care professionals. *Milbank Quarterly*, **70** (1), 43.

PHLS (Public Health Laboratory Service) (1995) (Figure gained directly from them, address is included in the Notes for further research).

Slovic, P. (1987) Perception of risk. *Science*, **236**, 280–5.

Tschudin, V. (1992) *Ethics in Nursing: The Caring Relationship*, 2nd edn. Oxford: Butterworth Heinemann.

UKCC (1991) *Code of Professional Conduct*. (2nd edn) London: UK Central Council for Nursing and Midwifery.

CHAPTER 10

Notes for further research

Much information is written on the subjects of HIV and AIDS. On the specific subject of HIV and the infected health care worker the information is scattered throughout various papers, essays and official government documents. To my knowledge, at the time of writing, this book is the only one devoted to this subject and I have tried to include most of my research here. I would, however, encourage any student who wishes to know more about the subject to pursue research in the following suggested sources. The material written about HIV dates very quickly and new information and developments are occurring all of the time. Although the figures and statistics produced in this book were correct at the time of writing, I encourage anyone using this book for study or quotation to check current statistics.

Organizations that may be of help for further research and study are:

Information on clinical practice

UK Advisory Panel for Health Care Workers Infected with Blood-borne Viruses
c/o Secretariat
Room 727
Wellington House
135–155 Waterloo Road
London
SE1 8UG

Nursing Organizations

United Kingdom Central Council for Nursing, Midwifery and Health Visiting (UKCC)
23 Portland Place
London
W1N 3AF

Royal College of Nursing (RCN)
20 Cavendish Square
London
W1M 0AB

English National Board (ENB) for Nursing, Midwifery and Health Visiting
Victory House
170 Tottenham Court Road
London W1P CM3

Policy documents and Department of Health guidelines

BAPS
Health Publications Unit
DSS Distribution Centre
Heywood Stores
Manchester Road
Heywood
Lancashire
OL10 2PS

Legal advice

Immunity
1st Floor
32–38 Osnaburgh Street
London
NW1 3ND

Transmission data

Public Health Laboratory Service (PHLS)
Communicable Disease Surveillance Centre
61 Colindale Avenue
London
NW9 5EQ

Support for HIV-infected health care workers

Give Way
Information and support for HIV-infected health care workers
Information by telephone only. No address.
Mondays 5 to 7 p.m., Tel 01293 562086.

Representatives of those infected

UK Coalition of People Living with HIV and AIDS
Southbank House
Black Prince Road
Albert Embankment
London
SE1 7SJ

Internet and Compuserve also offer access to information. I can recommend *Health Database Plus*.

General

Terrence Higgins Trust (THT)
52–54 Grays Inn Road
London
WC1X 8JU
Tel: 0171 831 0330

THT have a very good library of HIV-related information and the staff are very helpful. Appointments must be booked in advance. There are photocopying facilities and a very comprehensive newspaper cuttings library. They also have a CD-ROM of in-house information.

APPENDIX A

DEPARTMENT OF HEALTH *GUIDANCE ON THE MANAGEMENT OF HIV-INFECTED HEALTH CARE WORKERS*

The guidance relevant to HIV-infected health care workers in the past has been blamed for problems that have arisen when workers have presented themselves to the relevant authorities with an HIV diagnosis. I believe it is true to say that in the past they have been a problem, though the latest guidelines do seem to be fairer. Even if the guidelines are suspect in places the prejudices and attitudes of those interpreting them are even more in need of attention. It would seem that HIV-infected health care workers are more at risk of falling foul of others' beliefs, however misinformed, than they are of the guidelines themselves. The guidelines are presented here as an overview with brief explanations.

The Department of Health published its latest guidelines on the management of HIV-infected health care workers in March 1994 and at the time of writing (May 1996) they were still current, although from time to time minor changes are made. When they were published, Lady Cumberlege, Health Minister, said that 'The revised guidelines aim to strike the best possible balance between the need to provide reassurance to patients that they are not being placed at risk, while protecting the confidentiality and employment rights of the health care workers.' (Department of Health press release, 21 March 1994).

The Guidance is quite lengthy, comprising more than 4000 words. The Department of Health has produced a summary in the form of 16 points which are called key recommendations. These key recommendations provide a useful and concise overview of the Guidance.

1. The majority of procedures in the health care setting pose no risk of transmission of the Human Immunodeficiency Virus (HIV) and the risk of transmission from health care workers is considered remote (Paragraph 1.3).

This first point of the key recommendations is really a statement. It states that the guidelines are based on the fact that the risks of transmission from an HIV-infected health care worker to a patient are confined to a small number of procedures and that the risk of transmission during one of these procedures is unlikely.

2. Provided general infection control measures are followed scrupulously, the circumstances in which HIV could be transmitted from a health care worker to a patient are restricted to exposure prone procedures in which injury to the health care worker could result in the worker's blood contaminating the patient's open tissue. Such procedures must not be performed by an HIV infected health care worker (Paragraphs 3.2 and 3.4).

Point 2 is the linchpin. It states that although the risk to patients from HIV-infected care workers is small, there does, however, remain a hypothetical potential risk. Therefore, anyone known to be HIV-positive should abstain from exposure-prone procedures. This is because it is thought that accidents during 'exposure-prone procedures' are the most likely possibility of HIV transmission from a worker to a patient. However, it must be pointed out that there are many health care workers and involved in exposure-prone procedures who are unaware of their status and yet to date no one has been infected in this way. But for the Department of Health any risk of transmission regardless of how improbable, is too risky. For this reason the guidance further requires:

3. All health care workers are under an overriding ethical as well as legal duty to protect the health and safety of their patients. Those who believe they may have been exposed to infection with HIV, in whatever circumstances, must seek medical advice and diagnostic HIV antibody testing if appropriate (Paragraph 4.2).

Point three is a reminder of the ethical and legal duty health care workers have to protect the health and safety of patients. If health care workers believe they have been exposed to the HIV virus, they must seek medical advice and diagnostic testing. The duty to ensure the safety of the patient overrides the hypothetical risk.

How does one assess the risk of possibly being exposed to the virus? You could go as far as to say that anyone who has had penetrative sex without a condom in the last 15 years is potentially at risk.

The Department of Health, in the complete text of the Guidance, states that any policy that compels 'groups of individuals to be tested for HIV infection is regarded as discriminatory, interferes with individuals' rights and may deter those who are most in need of education and counselling from seeking advice'. Being homosexual is not reason enough to consider having put oneself at risk. One is at risk from the transmission routes of HIV and not from belonging to certain groups. The Declaration of the Rights of People with HIV and AIDS issued by the National AIDS Trust states that: 'In respect of the right to work, the right to privacy, and the right to protection from discrimi-nation, there should be no obligation or requirement upon an individual to disclose to an employer their own HIV status, or the HIV status of another person.'

Point three seems to state that the Department of Health expects health care workers to sacrifice this right because of their obligation to the health and safety of the patient. The Guidance asks us to remember that responsibility when considering a test. It supports that health care workers have a moral responsibility as well as a legal responsibility.

4. Health care workers who are infected with HIV must seek appropriate expert medical and also occupational health advice. Those who perform or who may be expected to

perform exposure-prone procedures must obtain further expert advice about the need for modification or restriction of their work practices. If exposure-prone procedures are being performed, these activities must cease whilst expert advice is sought (Paragraphs 4.3 and 6.1).

This point can be linked in with point 2 – that HIV-infected health care workers must not carry out exposure-prone procedures. If HIV-infected health care workers are to be stopped from carrying out these procedures the occupational health service needs to know about their HIV status. This definitely constitutes an obligation to tell one's employer. As was stated earlier, the Declaration of the Rights of People Infected with HIV and AIDS states that this is an infringement of the right to work and the right to privacy. However, most people who are HIV-positive do not have to carry out exposure-prone procedures in their daily jobs, nor do most people working with patients incur an ethical or legal duty to ensure their patients' safety at all times.

It seems that health care workers are a different case and that special rules apply only because of the exceptional nature of their work, i.e. exposure-prone procedures and the potential risk of transmission, not because of discrimination against individuals or those groups primarily affected.

5. HIV infected health care workers who do not perform exposure-prone procedures but who are involved with clinical care of patients must remain under regular medical and occupational health supervision and receive appropriate occupational health advice if their circumstances change (Paragraph 4.4).

HIV-infected health care workers, even if they are not involved in exposure-prone procedures, have an ethical duty to tell the occupational health department. This is because the working circumstances of a health care worker might change, e.g. the HIV-infected health care worker may pursue a job that involves exposure-prone procedures, which as we know is unethical because of the hypothetical potential risk.

6. If it is clear that if exposure-prone procedures have been performed, the infected health care worker [employed in England and Wales] should inform the local Director of Public Health (DPH), (if employed in Scotland, the Chief Administrative Medical Officer, CAMO) on a strictly confidential basis. The health care worker may however request that a physician acting on his/her behalf should inform the DPH or CAMO who should consult the UK Advisory Panel before proceeding (Paragraph 4.5).

As exposure-prone procedures are considered to be the only potential risk in the transmission of HIV from a health care worker to a patient, it follows that the local DPH need only ne informed if an HIV-infected health care worker has carried out these procedures. He does not need to be informed if the worker has not been involved in exposure-prone procedures. If the HIV-infected health care worker has not sought or followed advice, then physicians or occupational health practitioners are obligated to inform the appropriate body.

7. Physicians or occupational health practitioners who are aware that infected health care workers have not sought or followed advice to modify their practice, and/or are

continuing to perform exposure prone procedures, should inform the regulatory body as appropriate and also the DPH or CAMO in confidence (Paragraph 4.6).

8. Health Authorities (HAs), NHS Trusts (NHSTs) and Family Health Services Authorities (FHSAs) [In Scotland, Health Boards (HBs) and in Northern Ireland, Health and Social Services Boards (HSSBs)] and all other employers (including independent contractors and visiting health care workers) [must publicize] professional regulatory bodies' notices of ethical responsibilities and occupational guidance for AIDS–HIV infected health care workers (Paragraph 5.1).

Point 8 is an attempt to ensure that those working in whatever capacity in the health care profession are aware of what is expected of them. The Guidance appeals to one's moral integrity to have a test if one believes oneself to have been exposed to HIV in whatever circumstances.

9. All students in training must have the relevant professional statements brought to their attention by medical, dental, nursing and midwifery colleges and universities (Paragraph 5.3).

Point 9 states that students are subject to the same rules as qualified health care workers. The competency of a worker can only be based effectively on receipt of a certificate or a passed exam. So does this mean that patients are at more risk from an HIV-infected health care worker who is unqualified? Once again, I repeat that there must be many health care students who are infected with HIV who have not infected anyone during clinical practice, a reflection of the minimal level of risk. However, an HIV-positive diagnosis for any health care worker would have implications for their future career.

10. Where an employer or member of staff (including those in HAs, NHSTs and FHSAs/HBs/HSSBs) is aware of the health status of a health care worker, there is a duty of confidence which requires that they should keep any such information confidential (Paragraph 5.3).

Confidentiality is such a central issue that a whole chapter is devoted to it (Chapter 6). The Guidance reminds us of that duty of confidentiality.

11. Employers must make every effort to arrange suitable alternative work and retraining opportunities, or where appropriate, early retirement, for HIV infected health care workers, in accordance with good general principles of occupational health practice (Paragraph 5.4).

Point 11 is an attempt to protect the rights of the worker. If the effect of disclosing one's HIV status to an employer was to further damage one's career, then it is certain that few would come forward. Point 11 states that attempts will be made to protect the employment rights of health care workers who come forward. This could be done by retraining or by moving the health care worker to a job that does not include exposure-prone procedures.

The only issue that gives cause for great concern is compulsory early retirement. This, as discussed earlier, is certainly open to abuse.

12. All matters arising from and relating to the employment of HIV infected health care workers should be coordinated through a specialist health physician (Paragraph 6.1).

Point 12 places the responsibilities arising from the employment of HIV-infected health care workers clearly with someone who is a specialist in HIV matters. Only someone who is correctly informed of the transmission risks that exist is able to make the right decision when it comes to someone's future career.

13. Those seeking the advice of the UK Advisory Panel for Health Care Workers Infected with Blood-borne Viruses should ensure the anonymity of the referred health care worker (Paragraph 7.2 and Annex B).

14. The Expert Advisory Group on AIDS and the UK Advisory Panel recommend that all patients who have undergone an exposure-prone procedure where the infected health care worker (including students) was the sole or a main operator should, as far as is practicable, be notified of this (Paragraph 8.1).

15. Every effort should be made to avoid disclosure of the worker's identity, or information which would allow deductive disclosure (Paragraph 10.2).

16. The fact that the infected worker may have died, or may have already been identified publicly, does not mean that the duties of confidentiality are at an end by reason of that fact alone (Paragraph 10.4).

The last four points refer back to the question of confidentiality. Point 14 gives some indication of possible action that may be taken if an HIV-infected health care worker is known to have carried out exposure-prone procedures. This is called a 'look-back exercise' and often results in a breach of confidentiality. This is not because of bad practice by health authorities, but because reporters who have an interest in the subject have ways of discovering identities. Confidentiality is breached through the offer of money or aggressive research under the guise of investigative journalism.

The Department of Health Guidance attempts to reflect both the ethical responsibility to protect the patient although the risks are minuscule, and the employment and privacy rights of HIV-infected health care workers. It is true that some of the points of the 'key recommendations' seem severe when it comes to basic rights. But health care workers are duty bound to follow strict ethical and legal codes, and these seem to justify the diminution of the rights afforded health care workers. Even though the risk of HIV transmission from an HIV-infected health care worker is almost non-existent, there does however remain a potential risk. Of course, if one was unaware of one's status, or was aware but had not followed the guidelines and had not notified the appropriate authorities and went on to infect someone, that individual would be solely accountable. In effect, the Department of Health can be accountable only for known HIV-positive health care workers who have followed the Guidance. All other responsibilities are down to individual health care workers.

The complete text of the guidance is available from:

BAPS
Health Publications Unit
DSS Distribution Centre
Heywood Stores
Manchester Road
Heywood
Lancashire
OL10 2PA

APPENDIX B

UKCC *POSITION STATEMENT ON HIV-INFECTED HEALTH CARE WORKERS*
Reproduced with the kind permission of the UKCC

Introduction

1. In March 1988 the council released its first statement on 'AIDS and HIV Infection'. That statement emphasized the importance of good standards of practice in all circumstances and set out for those who employ nurses, midwives and health visitors the Council's position concerning the management of staff known to be infected with the virus. It was also intended to contribute to dispelling the mythology that is associated with this subject. In the light of developments since the statement was issued and the continued misrepresentation of facts concerning the infection, that original statement has been revised on a number of occasions. The contents of this paper are directed to registered nurses, midwives and health visitors, those who employ them and any other interested persons.

The Council's Code of Professional Conduct

2. The 'Code of Professional Conduct for the Nurse, Midwife and Health Visitor' is a statement to the profession of the primacy of interests of individual patients and clients. It goes on to indicate to all persons on the register maintained by the Council that, in the exercise of their personal accountability, they must '. . . act always in a such a manner as to promote and safeguard the interests and well-being of patients and clients'.

3. The Code of Professional Conduct emphasizes, therefore, the ethical imperative faced by each individual nurse, midwife and health visitor to serve the interests of patients and clients through their decisions and actions.

The Council's Position in Respect of routine HIV Testing of Health Care Professions.

4. The Council is opposed to the introduction of routine testing for registered nurses, midwives and health visitors and other health care workers. Its reasons for such opposition are that:

4.1 it would generate a false sense of security;

4.2 it might lead practitioners to allow standards of personal practice to fall should they quite falsely believe no HIV seropositive practitioner to be present and

4.3 given the seroconversion time between acquisition of the infection and the appearance of antibodies in the blood, even frequently repeated testing at great expense could not guarantee that, at the operative time, the practitioners involved in the care of patients are not infected. Similarly, routine testing of patients will provide no guarantee that they are not infected.

5. The Council's position is therefore based on achieving security through safe standards of practice at all times. The current assessment is that this needs to be supplemented by the appropriate re-assignment of practitioners known to be infected with HIV if their role involves the performance of exposure-prone procedures or they (the practitioners) need protection from the risk of other infection. Exposure-prone procedures are defined in paragraph 10.

Means of Transmission
6. The means of transmission of the Human Immuno-deficiency Virus (HIV) are well established. Three modes of transmission only have been identified. These are:

6.1 sexual intercourse (heterosexual or homosexual);

6.2 blood, blood products, donated organs and semen

6.3 mother to child transmission before or during birth and through breast feeding.

There is no evidence to indicate that HIV infection can be transmitted by respiratory or enteric routes, or by casual person-to-person contact in any social, domestic, work, school, hospital, prison or other settings.

Avoiding Infection and Spread of Infection
7. The occupational risk of HIV transmission from practitioner to patient is very remote in any event, but negligible if appropriate practice methods and strategies are diligently followed. Such precautions amount to no more than the good clinical practice which all practitioners have a responsibility to maintain in all situations, irrespective of their serological status any knowledge they may have of their patients. All blood and body fluids pose a potential infection risk and appropriate precautions must be taken. A number of Public Health Laboratory Service publications issued in October 1993 address this subject.[1, 2, 3]

8. Safety comes through recognizing that all practitioners, like all patients, pose a potential infection risk, and all must ensure that high standards of clinical practice are maintained. The promotion of these standards is an essential task for clinical and educational staff, managers and individual practitioners.

9. Such standards require that if a nurse, midwife or health visitor is infected with HIV, she or he must take appropriate precautions to eliminate any possibility of blood or body fluid contamination to a patient. This necessitates the use of appropriate precautions to prevent transmission of any infections to a patient and may, in some instances, require re-assignment of the practitioner to a different area of professional practice. Since the available evidence

indicates that the major route of occupational acquired HIV infection is through needle stick injuries, good practice must be employed to minimize the risk of such injury.

The Role and Responsibilities of the Occupational Health Service

10. The document entitled 'Guidance on the Management of HIV Infected Health Care Workers' produced by the UK Department of Health includes a sequence of paragraphs regarding the role of the occupational health service in this context. The paragraphs emphasize the full range of support and the strict standards of confidentiality which can be expected from such a service. The importance of maintaining confidentiality cannot be overstated. This applies to health care workers as much as to any other people consulting registered health care professionals. It is accepted, however, that there will be rare occasions on which professional practitioners in Occupational Health, faced with an HIV positive practitioner engaged in exposure prone procedures who is not complying with specialist advice to change her or his area of practice, may deem it necessary to communicate information concerning the practitioner's HIV status to the appropriate medical practitioner of the employing authority in confidence and to the individual's professional regulatory body. Exposure-prone procedures are defined by the UK Health Department as follows:

> Exposure prone procedures are those where there is a risk that injury to the worker may result in the exposure of the patient's open tissues to the blood of the worker. These procedures include those where the worker's gloved hands may be in contact with sharp instruments, needle tips or sharp tissues (spicule of bone or teeth) inside a patient's open body cavity or confined anatomical space where the hands or fingertips may not be completely visible at all times.[4]

A similar guidance document states that 'such procedures must not be performed by a health care worker who is either HIV positive or Hepatitis B e antigen positive.[5]

The Management of the Nurse, Midwife and Health Visitor who is HIV Positive

11. Some employers will become aware of a situation in which a nurse, midwife or health visitor has developed AIDS, has an HIV related illness or is HIV positive but not presenting symptoms. In determining their response to such a situation, employers should note the means of transmission stated in paragraph 6 above. Employers should also have regard to the information and guidance, particularly that concerning 'Exposure-prone Procedures', contained in the publication *AIDS-HIV Infected Health Care Workers: Guidance on the Management of Infected Health Care Workers*, issued by the UK Health Department in March 1994.

The Responsibility of the Employer

12. Occasionally information that a practitioner is infected with HIV will be provided by that employee to their employer. Given knowledge of the means of transmission, there is no reason to dismiss or suspend such an employee on the grounds that they pose an unacceptable infection risk to patients. To simply remove the known HIV positive health care worker, but fail to address the standards of practice, promotes a false sense of security and is discriminatory and counter productive.

This particular role and functions of the infected person must be considered. Where she or he is involved in performing exposure prone procedures, remote though the risk of practitioner to patient transmission is, re-assignment to an alternative area of practice will be regarded by that person's specialist medical advisor as necessary.

The Responsibility of Individual Practitioners with HIV Infection

13. Although the risk of transmission of HIV infection from a practitioner to a patient is remote, and, on the available evidence much less than the risk of patient to practitioner transmission, the risk must be taken seriously. The UK Department of Health has commissioned a study to evaluate the risk. It is incumbent on the person who is HIV positive to ensure that she or he is assessed regularly by medical advisors and complies with the advice received.

14. Similarly, a nurse, midwife or health visitor who believes that she or he may have been exposed to infection with HIV, in whatever circumstances, should seek specialist medical advice and diagnostic testing, if applicable. She or he must then adhere to the specialist medical advice received. Each practitioner must consider very carefully their professional accountability as defined in the Council's Code of Professional Conduct and remember that she or he has an overriding ethical duty of care to patients.

The Need to Disseminate Information and Avoid Discrimination

15. Prevention of the spread of HIV infection is important and is largely dependent on the dissemination of accurate information. Information and education programmes can only succeed if there is a supportive social environment and relevant health sources available. Such a supportive environment manifests tolerance rather than discrimination. Discrimination undermines the information and education programme and, in this context, endangers public health. It is the responsibility of every registered nurse, midwife and health visitor to be well informed and equipped to disseminate accurate information and eliminate the mythology surrounding this infection.

AIDS: Testing, Treatment and Care of Patients and Clients

16. On the specific issue of the taking of blood for testing without consent, the Council advises all its practitioners that they expose themselves to the possibility of criminal charges or of complaint to their regulatory body (the Council) alleging misconduct if they personally take blood specimens, or if they cooperate in obtaining such specimens. Informed consent is regarded as essential prior to such testing.

Justified Exceptions to Consented Testing of Patients and Clients

17. The Council accepts, however, that there might possibly be rare and exceptional circumstances when unconsented testing may legitimately occur. These must be able to be justified as in the interests of the particular patient at the operative time, and for no other reason, and only when it is not possible to obtain consent. In adopting this position the Council recognizes that improved forms of treatment are now available which, while not offering the prospect of cure, ameliorate the symptoms and assist the quality of remaining life for infected persons.

Anonymous Prevalence Monitoring for Epidemiological Purposes

18. The only other exception would be a situation in which, blood having been taken for the purpose of tests ordered by the patient's medical practitioner, the residue of the specimen is rendered anonymous and included in a programme of unlinked testing for HIV approved by the local research ethics committee as part of approved prevalence testing within the wider national programme. For information in respect of the anonymous prevalence monitoring programme see the Council position statement on 'Anonymous Testing for Prevalence of the Human Immuno-deficiency Virus (HIV) Infection'.

Non-discriminatory Care

19. In respect of other aspects of the treatment and care of patients known to be or suspected of being infected with the Human Immuno-deficiency Virus, the council reminds those on its register that clauses 1, 2 and 7 of its Code of Professional Conduct set out criteria against which allegations of misconduct are judged. They are not a formula for a practitioner to be selective about the categories of patient for whom she or he will or will not care.

Enquiries about this Statement

20. Enquiries in respect of this statement should be directed to the Assistant Registrar, Standards and Ethics, telephone number (071) 637–7181, extension 241.

Notes

1. 'Surveillance of occupational exposure to HIV: information for health care workers and their carers', Public Health Laboratory Service AIDS Centre at the Communicable Diseases Surveillance Centre, October 1993.
2. 'Exposure to blood and body fluids in the workplace: information for health care workers', Public Health Laboratory Service AIDS Centre at the Communicable Diseases Surveillance Centre, October 1993.
3. 'Health care workers and HIV: surveillance of occupationally acquired infection in the United Kingdom', Public Health Laboratory Service AIDS Centre at the Communicable Diseases Surveillance Centre, October 1993.
4. Extract from 'Guidance on the Management of HIV Infected Health Care Workers', issued by the UK Department of Health, March 1994.
5. 'Protecting health care workers and patients from Hepatitis B', UK Health Department, August 1993.

APPENDIX C

UKCC *CODE OF PROFESSIONAL CONDUCT, 1992* (3rd edn)
Reproduced with the kind permission of the UKCC

Notice to all Registered Nurses, Midwives and Health Visitors
This Code of Professional Conduct for the Nurse, Midwife and Health Visitor is issued to all registered nurses, midwives and health visitors by the United Kingdom Central Council for Nursing, Midwifery and Health Visiting. The Council is the regulatory body responsible for the standards of these professions and it requires members of the professions to practise and conduct themselves within the standards and framework provided by the Code.

Each registered nurse, midwife and health visitor shall act, at all times, in such a manner as to:

- safeguard and promote the interests of individual patients and clients;
- serve the interest of society;
- justify public trust and confidence and
- uphold and enhance the good standing and reputation of the professions.

As a registered nurse, midwife or health visitor, you are personally accountable for your practice and, in the exercise of your professional accountability, must:

1. act always in such a manner as to promote and safeguard the interests and well-being of patients and clients;
2. ensure that no action or omission on your part, or within your sphere of responsibility, is detrimental to the interests, condition or safety of patients and clients;
3. maintain and improve your professional knowledge and competence;
4. acknowledge any limitations in your knowledge and competence and decline any duties or responsibilities unless able to perform them in a safe and skilled manner;
5. work in an open and co-operative manner with patients, clients and their families, foster their independence and recognize and respect their involvement in the planning and delivery of care;

6. work in a collaborative and co-operative manner with health professionals and others involved in providing care, and recognize and respect their particular contributions within the care team;

7. recognize and respect the uniqueness and dignity of each patient and client, and respond to their need for care, irrespective of their ethnic origin, religious beliefs, personal attributes, the nature of their health problems or any other factor;

8. report to an appropriate person or authority, at the earliest possible time, any conscientious objection which may be relevant to your professional practice;

9. avoid any abuse of your privileged relationship with patients and clients and of the privileged access allowed to their person, property, residence or workplace;

10. protect all confidential information concerning patients and clients obtained in the course of professional practice and make disclosures only with consent, where required by the order of a court or where you can justify disclosure in the wider public interest;

11. report to an appropriate person or authority, having regard to the physical, psychological and social effect on patients and clients, any circumstances in the environment of care which could jeopardize standards of practice;

12. report to an appropriate person or authority any circumstances in which safe and appropriate care for patients and clients cannot be provided;

13. report to an appropriate person or authority where it appears that the health or safety of colleagues is at risk, as such circumstances may compromise standards of practice and care;

14. assist professional colleagues, in the context of your own knowledge, experience and sphere of responsibility, to develop their professional competence, and assist others in the care team, including informal carers, to contribute safely and to a degree appropriate to their roles;

15. refuse any gift, favour or hospitality from patients or clients currently in your care which might be interpreted as seeking to exert influence to obtain preferential consideration and

16. ensure that your registration status is not used in the promotion of commercial products or services, declare any financial or other interests in relevant service and ensure that your professional judgment is not influenced by any commercial considerations.

The Council's Code is kept under review and any recommendations for change and improvement would be welcomed and should be addressed to the:

Registrar and Chief Executive
United Kingdom Central Council for Nursing, Midwifery and Health Visiting
23 Portland Place
London
W1N 3AF

APPENDIX D

UK ADVISORY PANEL FOR HEALTH CARE WORKERS INFECTED WITH BLOOD-BORNE VIRUSES
GENERAL COUNTER INFECTION MEASURES FOR THE CLINICAL SETTING

(*Guidance for Clinical Health Care Workers: Protection Against Infection with HIV and Hepatitis Viruses*. Reproduced with kind permission of the Department of Health.)

The primary measures for prevention of occupational 'exposure' to HIV and blood-borne hepatitis viruses in the health care setting are:

 i) protection of existing wounds, skin lesions, conjunctivae and mucosal surfaces and the prevention of puncture wounds, cuts and abrasions in the presence of blood and body fluids;

 ii) the application of simple protective measures designed to avoid contamination of the person or clothing with blood and good basic hygiene practices including regular hand washing;

 iii) control of work surface contamination by blood and body fluids by containment and disinfection;

 iv) avoidance of sharps usage where possible but when their use is essential, the exercising of particular care in handling and disposal; and

 v) safe disposal of contaminated waste.

The successful implementation of these measures necessitates:

 i) assessing the particular occupational risks and ensuring suitable measures are used to minimize exposures. This will include a consideration of the risks to others such as in the disposal of bodies, tissues, body fluids, contaminated consumables and sharps and in the maintenance of equipment;

 ii) devising safe, reasonably practicable procedures and routines for performing each task; ensuring that they are followed and actively keeping them under review;

iii) promoting an awareness of risks by providing information and training; and

iv) reviewing accidents in which an exposure occurs and considering how to prevent recurrences.

Assessments of risks associated with clinical tasks

This section provides a framework for assessing the risk of clinical work practices in the context of transmission of HIV and hepatitis viruses. It is intended only as a general guide. The central consideration in the assessment is the extent to which a health care worker carrying out or assisting with a procedure is likely to be exposed to blood.

A suggested means of task categorization is as follows:

A. Risk of exposure to blood.
  i) Contact of health care worker with blood probable with potential for bleeding or spattering.
  ii) Contact of health care worker with blood probable but spattering unlikely.
  iii) Low probability of personal contact with blood, any unexpected blood flow readily contained.
B. No risk of exposure to blood.

Precautions to be adopted

Tasks in category A(i) will include most major surgical, gynaecological and obstetric procedures and require as high a level of protective measures as is practicable. The level of precautions should generally include use of the following:

Gloves
Water repellent gowns and aprons
Protective headwear
Masks
Protective eyewear
Protective footwear

In addition to these appropriate washing facilities including eyewash should be at hand in case of accident. It is imperative that protective clothing be removed on leaving the contaminated area. This is particularly important for contaminated footwear since blood is readily disseminated unwittingly by this means. All contaminated reusable protective clothing must be subjected to cleaning and disinfection/sterilization with appropriate precautions for those undertaking it.

Tasks in category A(ii) require the use of gloves as a minimum level of protection. Examples from the general clinical setting are intra-arterial punctures and insertion and removal of standard intravenous and intra-arterial lines. Additional measures such as facial protection will be required for some tasks, e.g. removal of 'long lines' where there is a risk of localized splashing, but the full range of measures recommended above for category A(i) tasks would not generally be warranted.

Tasks in category A(iii) will normally not require use of protective measures but gloves of an appropriate standard should be readily available in case it becomes necessary to staunch unexpected blood flow. An example of such a task is the administration of intramuscular, subcutaneous or intradermal injections. For tasks such as removal of soiled dressings, appropriate hygienic precautions should be adopted and a 'no touch' technique used by the health care worker.

In some cases, the decision to allocate a task within category A will depend on the skill and technique of the health care worker and the circumstances in which the procedure is carried out. A specific example is venepuncture where it is recommended that gloves be worn if the venepuncturist is inexperienced or has cuts or abrasions on the hands, such that it is not practical for them to be covered in waterproof dressings alone. Gloves should also be worn if the patient is restless or if the patient is known to be infected with HIV or hepatitis viruses.

Workers not directly involved in clinical procedures may nevertheless be exposed to blood, e.g. when cleaning patients after surgery or childbirth or when cleaning equipment or operating theatres. It is essential that they be provided with suitable protective clothing including where necessary, forearm, facial and foot protection.

Tasks in category B, which excludes contact with blood but includes possible exposure to body fluids such as urine, faeces, etc., require no specific precautions for prevention of transmission of HIV and the blood-borne hepatitis viruses unless these fluids are visibly contaminated with blood. However, good general hygienic precautions including regular hand washing should always apply and considerations of general infection control will often dictate the use of further protective measures.

Guidance common to all areas of practice

Many accidental exposures to blood-borne pathogens result from failure to adhere to basic rules concerning decontamination, waste disposal, etc., and the following general guidance should be drawn to the attention of ALL STAFF within their employment setting. Moreover, it is desirable for there to be a designated individual who has responsibility for ensuring that guidance on sterilization and disinfection and clinical waste disposal is adhered to. This is particularly important in order to protect third parties, often ancillary staff, from preventable exposure.

Equipment and materials

Wherever possible single-use equipment and materials should be employed in clinical procedures. This is particularly important if a patient is known or suspected to be infected with HIV or hepatitis viruses. Any equipment which is to be reused and which has been employed for a procedure involving potential contact with a patient's blood must be sterilized or disinfected. Such equipment includes items which may not necessarily be in direct contact with the patient, e.g. manual self-inflating resuscitation bags and dental hand pieces. Reusable equipment must be of type that is easily decontaminated without distortion or damage to its function and the manufacturers' instructions must be consulted to ensure compatibility of materials with the methods of contamination employed.

When selecting suction and aspiration equipment, apparatus which will discharge directly into a waste outlet is to be preferred in order to reduce the potential for accidental spillage. High speed aspirators used for dentistry should exhaust externally in order to avoid the spread of potentially infectious material within the surgery.

Disposal of clinical waste (excluding sharps)

All waste which is contaminated with blood must be considered as potentially infective and treated as clinical waste. Attention is drawn to the duties of the employer under the Health and Safety at Work etc. Act 1974 which extends to employees working in the home environment. Thus the employer must ensure that adequate arrangements are made for disposal of clinical waste in the community as well as in the hospital situation.

Disposal of sharps

Surgical or other single-use gloves cannot protect workers from sharps injuries. This underlines the need for extreme care in both the use and disposal of sharps since the circumstances in which many such injuries are sustained are easily avoided. In particular, other staff must not be put at risk by careless disposal of sharps and all workers must be reminded of their responsibilities in this context.

Used needles must not be re-sheathed unless there is a safe means available for doing so. Needles should only be removed from syringes when essential, e.g. when transferring blood to a container, and needle forceps or other suitable devices should be readily available. All disposable sharps must be promptly placed in a secure puncture-resistant bin suitable for incineration and which is sited out of the reach of children. These bins must never be overfilled since used needles protruding from overloaded containers constitute a very significant hazard to those who handle them. The size of items to be disposed of in sharps bins will vary considerably and it is essential that bins of adequate capacity be provided. When syringes containing arterial blood are to be sent to the laboratory, needles must be removed and blind hubs attached to the syringes. Intravascular guide wires and glass slides must be disposed of as sharps.

Non-disposable sharps should be placed in a suitable secure enclosure to await decontamination.

Contaminated linen

In the hospital setting linen contaminated with blood should be treated as 'infected linen'. It should be sealed in a water soluble bag, or one with a water soluble membrane, immediately on removal from the bed or before leaving the clinical department. This primary container should then be placed in a red or a red-marked nylon or polyester bag and labeled according to local procedures.

In the community, linen and bedding that is blood stained should be washed in a well maintained machine, rinsing initially in the cold rinse cycle and then in the hot wash cycle (at approximately 80°C). Overloading of the machine must be avoided. If washing by hand is unavoidable, household rubber gloves must be worn.

Labeling, transport and reception of specimens

Information about labeling, transport and reception of specimens was published by the Health Services Advisory Committee in 1986. When a specimen is known or suspected of containing HIV or HBV a warning label stating 'danger of infection' must be applied to both the request form and the specimen container. The securely closed specimen container must be placed in a sealed transparent plastic bag for transport. The request form must give sufficient information to the experienced laboratory staff who will receive it to know what special precautions are required in the laboratory.

Body handling and disposal

When there is a risk of contact with blood and body fluids, single use gloves must be worn and high standards of personal hygiene adopted. Drainage tube sites and open wounds must be covered by waterproof dressings and any body which is more generally contaminated with blood or any body known or suspected to be infected with HIV or hepatitis viruses must be placed in a disposable plastic body bag as soon as possible.

Wherever a person who is known or suspected to be HIV or hepatitis dies, it is essential that funeral personnel and all others involved in handling the body are informed of the potential risk of infection if there is contact with blood or body fluids.

The embalming of bodies which are known or suspected to be infected is not recommended but if judged to be essential, particular attention must be given to avoiding contamination and the work must be done by experienced staff wearing protective clothing. Mortuary staff should ensure that good liaison is maintained between themselves and those who submit bodies for postmortem examination and/or storage and those who collect bodies for disposal. Those undertaking postmortem examination must take the same precautions as are recommended in this document for invasive procedures on living patients. The postmortem examination of patients with AIDS or of others with known or suspected HIV or hepatitis infection must be undertaken only by a consultant pathologist with the assistance of experienced pathology technicians.

Index